READY ABOUT!

READY ABOUT!

GARRY HOYT

INTERNATIONAL MARINE PUBLISHING COMPANY
Camden, Maine

Typeset by Typeworks, Belfast, Maine
Printed and bound by BookCrafters, Chelsea, Michigan

Published by International Marine Publishing Company
21 Elm Street, Camden, Maine 04843
(207) 236-4342

Illustrations by Jim Sollers

Library of Congress Cataloging-in-Publication Data

Hoyt, Garry.
    Ready about!

    1. Sailing.   2. Sailboats.   I. Title.
GV811.H659 1986   797.1'24   86-15237
ISBN 0-87742-229-X

To Hovey T. Freeman, Jr., good friend and good sailor.
We sailed many happy miles together.
Hovey died before his time, but he would have liked this book,
and in many ways his bluff and explorative spirit prompted it.

Contents

Preface

This is a sailor's book for those who might fancy a chance to sail better. It is not a scientific book because I am not a scientist. Nor is it an engineering book, for the same reason. But consider those facts to be qualifiers rather than disqualifiers, because they set me free to eye the unproven, the unlikely, and the paths less traveled.

What you are about to read and see are a series of experienced surmises and experimental probes. It would be fair to call them dreams, but not to dismiss them as such, because I am not given to vague or impractical thoughts. My credentials are that I sail, design, and write better than most, and have separately proven those skills in highly competitive fields. I see no point in hypocritical humility about this, and after forty-five years of sailing, I've had ample time to collect my thoughts.

The only thing I am out to deny you is the complacency of a set mind. A situation analysis shows all is not well in the sailing world, and this suggests that past practices stand in need of review and refreshment. The book is a barrage of my ideas thereto. The hope and intent is to provoke some new action on the sailing scene, and for those who might care to contact me in that regard, I am available at One Harbor View Drive, Newport, Rhode Island 02840. Keep in mind that neither calm seas nor tame visions ever made a good sailor.

Garry Hoyt

ONE

The Diverging Dichotomy of Sailing

*H*aving just attended the major European boat shows, I can report that the demarcation is distinct. On the main floor you have the conventional sailboats—the sailboards and catamarans are sold on separate floors to separate audiences. In the case of Dusseldorf's massive presentation the sailboards have several separate buildings all to themselves. The crowd splits at the doorway; one group goes one way, the other, the other, and the twain do not meet.

The differences go deeper than mere sales locations. The conventional boats create a depressingly familiar display, because essentially it hasn't changed in the past twenty years. The boats are all white fiberglass sloops with aluminum masts and blue-blazered salesmen. Except for the banners and labels, the boats are indistinguishable from one another. If someone overnight shifted the Jeanneau boats to the Beneteau booth, nobody would blink an eye because nobody would see any difference. The conventional yachting scene is slavishly imitative and uniformly stodgy, characterized by a myopic obsession with concepts that are fifty years old.

Ah, but enter the boardsailing floors and the mood changes abruptly. Instantly you are surrounded by color, motion, sound, and excitement. The sails are brilliant splashes of lime green, cool coral, and hot pink, striped, paneled, and polka-dotted in every manner of pattern. The boards come in an amazing variety of sizes and shapes complete with startling graphics that range from flowers to pornographic phrases. The rigs are amazing technological feats—fully battened taut membranes that are as close to a bird's wing as you can imagine—and clearly represent the leading edge of sail technology today. A barrage of multiple screen images bombards you with action shots of young athletes vaulting over waves or bursting across the water at 30 knots.

There are blue jeans, bikinis, and a whole range of specialized clothing that has forced the development of new dry suits, wet suits, shoes, and sailing helmets.

Boardsailing has managed to capture—and give special character to—a completely separate lifestyle, and you can see the excitement on the faces of the crowd. I might add that the crowd averages some 20 years younger. It's a clear case of T-shirts versus stuffed shirts, and the T-shirts are winning.

Well, so what, you might say. All that demonstrates is diversity, and what's wrong with that?

The problem is not diversity—but divergent courses. The sailboards are on a path of dynamic development, best proved by the fact that they have grown in 15 years from a crazy idea to be the world's fastest and most popular sailboats. In contrast, conventional sailboats are on a path of constricted development, closely escorted by constipated design and steady sales decline.

Worst of all, there is disturbing evidence that the traditional organizations of the sailing establishment—yacht clubs, the International Yacht Racing Union in general and the USYRU in particular, the Offshore Racing Council (the custodian of the International Offshore Rule), etc.—have become negative rather than positive growth factors. Not intentionally of course, because few would question their devotion to cause. But their tactics have clearly missed the pulse of modern public interest. After all, in terms of new sailors created in the past 15 years, by far the best success stories belong to catamarans and sailboards, both of which were developed entirely *outside* the yachting establishment, which in fact specifically pooh-poohed them from day one. They were created by non-naval architects and sailed right off the beach with conspicuous disregard for the rules and traditions of yacht clubs and yachting. I suggest that the sailing establishment runs the risk of becoming irrelevant if it persists in remaining out of touch with the changing tones of public interest and present realities. One sector of sailing is growing and one sector is declining, so the declining sector would do well to study the growing sector and somehow try to get in step. The first lesson that such a review would provide is that the conventional sailing world cannot continue to push the same designs and the same organizational formats in the same way and hope for new improvement. The sailing establishment has been muddling along, nourished by the hope that today's boardsailors would somehow become tomorrow's conventional sailors. That is a delusion not supported by the facts, because today's conventional boats are imprisoned in dated designs that have little chance of ever attracting the boardsailors, who are bred to faster, more exciting expectations.

To see how far apart we presently are, let's imagine a visitor from outer space—or maybe just from another sport—and see how he would characterize the two increasingly separate worlds of sailing. Call them two categories of what their respective participants perceive to be fun. The first category is costly, complex, difficult to learn, restricted by rules, portrayed and perceived to be dangerous, involves a high degree of maintenance expense, basically shuns women, and is capable of speeds of up to 10 miles per hour. The second is colorful, simple, inexpensive, completely portable, perceived to be glamorous and exciting, requires no maintenance, closely involves women, and is capable of speeds over 35 miles per hour. Now then—which category is most likely to appeal to the new generation?

Speaking as one who has sailed for more than 45 years—having been schooled in strict one-design racing and having owned a 58-foot Alden schooner, a 52-foot Herreshoff ketch, and a wide variety of subsequent cruising boats—there is no doubt in my mind that if I were 16 years old I would opt for boardsailing on the simple grounds that it offers more speed, more girls, and more fun with less hassle. I can throw the board on my car, go anywhere in the country, and who needs a yacht club or any silly rules the net result of which is to keep boats slower than they can be.

It is of course completely predictable that the sailing establishment does not see this, because if anybody is set in their ways, the members of that establishment are. They see no need for change because they are quite content with what they have. The 45-year-old owner of a C&C 35 is not likely to shuck that lifestyle to take up boardsailing or catamarans, nor indeed should he have to. But the issue is which category of sailing will be selected by the new generation, which has a choice the older generation did not have. And the big challenge is to make these two separate worlds of sailing *converge* rather than diverge.

The changes must come in the designs, the organizational formats, the attitudes, and the image of the conventional sailing world, because it is the conventional sailing world that is mired in stagnant designs and outmoded policies. For example, competitive boardsailors—on top of their more advanced designs, as evidenced by greater speed and simplicity—have better coped with the new realities of professionalism and commercial sponsorship. While the racing sailing establishment struts and frets over protecting the illusion of its long-vanished virginity, sailboards have simply adapted to the times and turned both professionalism and commercial interest to the further development of their sport. Today's reality is that we have conventional racing sailors who are paid to sail better—and do so. The average weekend sailor has about as much chance sailing against these professionals as the average tennis player does against John McEnroe. So the sailing pros regularly carve up the amateurs in the one-design championships, and this has the first effect of steadily diminishing the ranks of these amateurs in what was once the primary seeding ground for young sailors. Meanwhile, sailing professionals are forced to disguise themselves as sailmakers pretending to be amateurs. Thus they are denied the full benefits of professional rewards, because the pretense of amateurism does not allow the open commercial support that is the only practical means of providing adequate professional prize money.

Conventional racing sailing staggers under the weight of this hypocrisy. We see sailboards and oceangoing multihulls surviving and prospering under the financial freedom of commercial sponsorship, while in contrast the establishment agonizes over the technicalities of the International Yacht Racing Union's Rule 26 and stumbles around trying to keep participants from wearing brand-name T-shirts or naming their boats after products. I say let's cut away the sham and get on with it. We can have professional events that will attract the best sailors, the best equipment, and the best sponsors. We can keep an amateur level of competition that will grow better because it is protected from weekend raiding by professionals. We can have open events in which everybody competes together. But what we cannot have is the continued hypocrisy of an indecisive middle course that is neither amateur in its scruples, nor professional in its rewards.

All of which means that it is high time that the sailing establishment gets down off its high horse and joins the real world. Golf and tennis and skiing have done so with no visible loss to their prestige, and great gain in their popularity.

I am not optimistic about the ability of the conventional sailing world to quickly adapt to the new realities. In the first place the sailboat industry is burdened with too many builders pushing too many similar designs into too tiny a market. The paucity of fresh ideas, ever higher prices, and an image of complexity give off a fishlike odor and predictably lose out to other activities in the public's eye. The solution is fewer builders producing newer designs for an expanded market, but this is not likely to happen because there is not sufficient economic impetus to make it happen. Actually, the biggest and most profitable businesses in the sailing world are the sailing publications, who paradoxically thrive on the same multiplicity of producers and manufacturers which makes it impossible for the industry to be efficient.

There is little point in railing at the sailing magazines for having the smarts to be on the better side of the business. Rather I would hope to prod the sailing magazines to use their greater financial resources to join with manufacturers in a policy of enlightened self interest—to do for the sport what the sport seems inherently incapable of doing for itself.

Yachting—conventional sailing—needs a new injection of excitement and design change if it hopes to attract new participants or qualify as an eventual alternative for the growing ranks of boardsailors. To shake the yachting establishment out of its daze I suggest the following steps to be organized by the sailing magazines, either jointly or separately:

1. Create a contest with a $100,000 cash prize for a sailboat that can be safely soloed from a dock around a triangular course and back by a complete amateur after one hour of instruction. Entrants in this contest must provide their prototype boat and instruction system, and the winner is to be picked in open competition by the sponsor. The reason this new boat is necessary is that present boats and instructional systems only reinforce the fears and complexities that are presently inhibiting sailing's growth. When you consider that an average person can solo an airplane after eight hours of instruction, it should clearly be possible to master the far simpler and safer process of a sailing solo in one hour. And there is no better way to attract new interest than with the quick reward of individual accomplishment. Making people learn to sail by putting them on a large boat with three other people and an instructor may be the most profitable way to run a sailing school, but it is a lousy way to attract large numbers of new enthusiasts. You hit a golf ball by yourself, you hit a tennis ball by yourself, and you learn to ski by yourself. Similarly, giving people the unique thrill of sailing by themselves is the best way initially to attract them to the sport.

2. Create a $1,000,000 prize—with commercial sponsors—for the first sailboat to break the 40-knot barrier. When the barrier is broken—as it quickly can be—move the contest up to 45 knots and keep it going. Make the contest a yearly event and heavily publicize the trials in order to begin to invest sailing with the speed image which is vital to new public interest. When you consider that six syndicates in the United States will come up with a total of at least $60,000,000 to pursue a one-tenth

of a knot increase in twelve-meter speed, we surely ought to be able to shake loose $1,000,000 to go four times as fast. This kind of prize money would for the first time really stimulate new innovative minds into sailing matters.

3. Develop sailing resorts. Here we should take a lesson from the skiing world. It should be possible in sailing—just as it is in skiing—for a beginner, a total outsider, to go to an attractive resort, rent the necessary equipment, and be guaranteed an authentic weekend sampling of the sport, complete with the accomplishment of a solo sail and an active social atmosphere. Critical to this resort concept is the development of new equipment as outlined in point number one, because it must be possible for the beginner to say back at the office Monday, "I sailed a boat this weekend—all by myself."

The development of ski resorts very quickly enabled that sport to reach outside itself and provide a convenient, enjoyable, nonintimidating sampling of the sport to literally anybody. This is not currently possible in the sailing world, where the yacht club format often raises artificial barriers of exclusivity that are the antithesis of friendly invitation. All too often the gesture of taking a person out sailing ends up being a demonstration of their total inadequacy on board, with a confusing separate language and a bewildering array of equipment. The winches take lines that are called sheets that must be turned around a certain way, and by the way, be careful how you do it or you'll lose a finger. The best course around this dilemma is to create a commercial format that unbends sailing in ways the establishment has not been able to. Today's sailing schools are a step in the right direction, but they tend to be too intent on teaching traditional sailing—which is too complex an array of skills. They are trying to create sailors who can qualify to race or cruise on establishment terms. We need simpler ways to turn people on to the simple joy of harnessing the wind on the water. It is only old equipment and the insistence on old ways that makes sailing so difficult. The necessary expediency of a commercial resort format should very quickly find the quickest and easiest way to link human interest to sailing. And just as the governor of New Hampshire is able to make an open invitation and say on television, "Come on up to New Hampshire and learn to ski," so should other governors be able to say, "Come on up and learn to sail." That kind of simple, easy recreational access to sailing is not now available—and without it new growth is painfully slow.

4. De-macho the sport. The continued failure of conventional sailing to attract women is a costly overlooking of over half of the population. By persistently projecting a dated image of macho toughness—which is unfortunately reflected by the reality of today's ocean racing—we have succeeded in convincing most women that sailing is not the sport for them. Being unencumbered by male egos, women seriously question the recreational value of something repeatedly shown to be cold, wet, costly, dangerous, and uncomfortable. Yet the most popular theme of sailboat magazine covers remains a group of grizzled males perched precariously on a bobbing rail, plowing stoically to windward through towering seas. Not a woman in sight, of course—they'd rather be playing golf or tennis. Who in their right minds wouldn't be?

By focusing on an aspect of sailing that registers only male achievement in an all-male atmosphere of danger and discomfort, the magazines do a continuous disservice to the growth potential of the sport. Let's wise up and lighten up as a first step toward getting women on board. It is supposed to be fun, and competitive events that lose sight of that do not deserve primary promotion. There is of course a place for those who prize adversity for its own sake and for those who insist on equating hardship with achievement. But that place should not be center stage if growth in sailing is the goal. It is not that rugged events like the Whitbread Round the World Race should be ignored. They have a legitimate claim to public interest, but only if they are balanced by more frequent coverage of more fun events to keep things in proper perspective.

While the foregoing remarks may seem to be oriented toward conventional racing sailboats versus sailboards, the much larger world of cruising boats is equally in crisis, although on a schedule of more delayed impact. Cruising design has unfortunately been largely a matter of "hand me down" thinking from racing design, a backward approach that has predictably yielded backward results. The criteria for successful racing designs and successful cruising designs are often diametrically opposed. Relying on the designers and organizers of racing to come up with appropriate cruising choices is a bit like turning over representation of the home construction industry to the gun lobby.

You may take it as Hoyt's law that no participation sport involving large expenditures of money can succeed without the active enthusiasm of women. Wives may let their husbands buy fishing rods or hunting rifles or golf clubs, but there is no way they will passively permit a $20,000, $50,000 or $100,000 chunk that has to come out of the family budget. This problem is more complex than just adding designer colors to the interiors. Women must be convinced to cease being disinterested spectators and become instead interested participants. This means design changes to make sailing easier and safer, with more fun and less work. Pretending that the work is fun will not do, because women don't buy that men-against-the-sea routine. Not when the same amount of money will get them a ski lodge or a cottage on Cape Cod.

Well now, having broadsided the sailing establishment, the sailing industry, the sailing schools, and the sailing media, is there anyone I missed?

Of course, just loosing fusillades is not the answer. I certainly can't change the sailing world singlehanded, and my family wonders why I persist in tilting at windmills. I do so because I love the sport, and I have undiminished faith in the ability of common sense eventually to elude the grasp of tired habits. Mark Twain said, "Loyalty to petrified opinion never yet freed a human soul." Similarly, loyalty to petrified opinions will not free sailing to achieve its fullest potential. One of the first things we learn as sailors is, when you keep getting headed, it's time to tack. So I say to the sailing world, "Ready about!"

T W O

Where Are We Now?

*H*aving signalled the crisis and laid down the challenge, it seems cowardly not to at least attempt a few answers. What I hope to do in this book is pry open the field of sailing to some new ingenuity by dispelling a portion of the hardy myths and institutionalized absurdities that have paralyzed progress. By reviewing how my own thoughts on design have developed, perhaps I can prod others to the kind of innovation the sailing scene so desperately needs. First attention will be paid in these pages to the area of speed, where conventional sailing has most conspicuously failed.

Some historical information is in order. "Sailing with the wind" is an elementary problem that was essentially solved when the first caveman bestriding a log on a lake raised a leafy branch and discovered he could go faster downwind. All sailing ships up to the clipper ships are derivatives of this simple fact—the more area presented to the wind, the more force gained in the direction of the wind. Square-riggers with crudely curved sails and enough hull in the water to resist sideward motion more than forward motion managed by angling their yards to sail as close as ninety degrees to the wind. That was a lot better than rowing, but half the compass was still inaccessible to them.

It is well to note that progress was steady and satisfactory up to this point. Crude rafts evolved to clumsy galleons, to swift clipper ships that swept across the seas at exciting speeds. But the clipper ships, for all their stately grace, could never go to windward, and this flaw seriously interfered with their commercial and military practicality. The steam engine entered that gap in the 1800s, first with paddlewheels and then—better—with screw propellers. By conferring to a ship the ability to go directly where it wanted to go, regardless of whether there was any wind or what its

7

direction might be, engine power rapidly replaced sail power in the navies and merchant fleets of the world.

In those days—and to this day—the pressure of ingenious minds was most intensely focused on commercial or military applications. Thus, after the introduction of the engine, sail was precipitously deposed from top-of-the-mind consideration by the world's best brains, and relegated to the considerably lower pressure atmosphere of a rich man's recreation. Denied the financial support and the practical performance criteria of commercial competition (getting as much cargo there at the best speed with the least chance of failure), sailing was easy prey to the relaxed standards and deviant strains of a leisurely gentleman's sport.

The mischief that is the first product of idle minds quickly manifested itself in the introduction of rules and restrictions to govern the design of racing sailboats. This effectively shackled what should have been the leading edge of the field to artificial considerations that had very little to do with the basic problem of sailing faster and more safely.

Not to say there was no progress. By the 17th century the fore-and-aft rig had begun to demonstrate that it was indeed possible to make way to windward. This improvement was not nearly enough to stave off the straight-line efficiency of the engine, but it did open up the other one hundred eighty degrees of the compass to sailors. Awkward gaff-riggers gradually gave way to tightly stayed sloops as sailors edged ever closer to the wind. All was not pure gain, because the sloop, while unquestionably superior to the square-rigger upwind, was slightly inferior offwind, an annoying lapse which was only compensated for by the use of the spinnaker, a large and fractious parachute device requiring the skilled use of many hands. The combination of sloop rig plus spinnaker quickly became the regimen for all racing yachts, but the complexity, fragility, and labor intensity of this arrangement drove sailing ever further from commercial application or popular acceptance by a large public.

The next step in sailing progress can be attributed largely to the advent of new materials. Fiberglass hulls, aluminum masts, stainless steel fittings, and synthetic cloth sails provided significant improvements over what had been previously possible with wood, iron, and canvas. These material gains were enough to politely excuse the pointed lack of accompanying progress in design. In effect, the sailing world re-equipped 1930 designs with new materials and proudly proclaimed the resulting one-and-a-half-knot gains in speed as "high tech." That sailing would settle for those pitiful increments on already poor performance—while aviation and land transportation were literally rocketing ahead—is evidence of the ossification that has afflicted the sport.

Where else in the sporting world would the press proclaim as "Grand Prix Racing" the sorry spectacle of twelve men slumped over a wet rail, slogging along at eight knots on a $200,000 object that is obsolete the next season?

Where else would men spend two million dollars to produce a "maxi" yacht requiring a crew of twenty-two men, which can't go as fast as a horse can trot and is less than half as fast as many small one-man sailboards costing less than two thousand dollars?

Where else would highly organized syndicates spend over one hundred million dollars in the hope of a one-tenth knot increase in speed in elegant twelve-meter dinosaurs, when an R&D program of one million dollars could quickly produce sailboats of five times the speed and one-quarter the cost?

Alice would have felt right at home in this Wonderland.

If a fraction of the energy and money that the sailing establishment has applied toward standing reason on its head could instead be shifted to the more sensible goal of swifter, simpler sailing, we would be today sailing ordinary cruising boats at twenty miles per hour, and extraordinary racing boats at forty miles per hour. The sailing speed record would be over fifty knots, and sailing would be perceived as a dynamic general sport instead of a complex and dangerous rich man's fancy.

The first step toward new progress is to relieve sailing of its burden of basic stupidities, many of which are encrusted in place as hallowed traditions.

THREE

The Problem

The problem is to get an object capable of carrying people to move faster through two fluids, being propelled by the upper while floating on the lower. Being fluids, the two mediums share similar characteristics, but the lower is some eight hundred times more dense than the upper.

It would seem, and experience shows, that the shapes that are efficient in air are also efficient in water. The profiles of modern keels and rudders can be seen to match closely the profiles of jet wings and rudders.

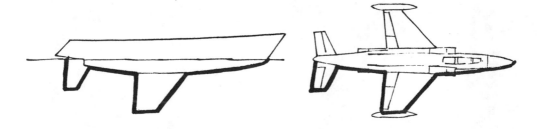

But while modern hulls have developed reasonable efficiency in the lower fluid, modern rigs remain hopelessly primitive in the upper fluid. For example, you could recreate the keel and rudder shape on deck, making the deck keel shape rotatable, and you would have a rig that would sail—admittedly slowly in light winds because the area is small, but quite efficiently in heavy winds.

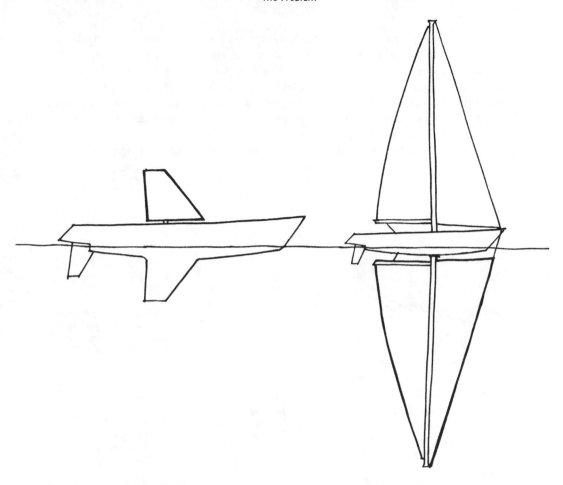

But if you tried to recreate the conventional stayed rig as an underwater shape, you would have an absolutely hopeless arrangement whose extreme drag would virtually prohibit forward motion. In fact, even if you tried to tow it with a powerful tug you'd be in trouble because of the overwhelming drag. Thus, inefficiencies that go unnoticed in the thin upper fluid are dramatically revealed in the dense lower fluid.

To appreciate the full extent of the drag problem, consider some more basic aerodynamic facts. In terms of developing lift (and minimizing drag) the following profile shapes are ranked in order of efficiency:

The triangular shape is conspicuously the worst shape available. Its triangular tip generates a continuous induced drag via a vortex effect. You can't see it, but it's there, slowing you down all the time. That is why you never see triangular tips on airplane wings, rudders, or stabilizers, and that is why you never see triangular keel tips or rudders on modern boats. Why then would designers prescribe for progress in the upper fluid the same inefficient triangular shape that they religiously reject for progress in the lower fluid? Dumb.

Let's study a further aerodynamic fact gleaned from a NASA article years ago.

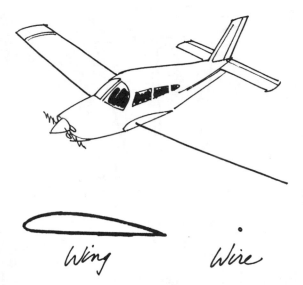

Wing   Wire

Consider, for example, the theoretical lightplane in the accompanying drawing. Its right wing is conventional, but the left consists only of a straight wire that has a diameter of one-half inch. Both "wings" have the same span.

It may seem incredible, but in cruise flight (if such a thing were possible), the slender wire would create as much parasitic drag as the entire wing on the other side.

If the conventional wing were perfectly clean and flawlessly built with a laminar-flow airfoil, then the wire would need to have only a one-quarter-inch diameter to create as much drag as the wing.

This tells us that parasitic drag is much more a function of shape than size. (The wing has a lot more mass than the wire, but their drag is equal.)

So we see that the triangular stayed sloop rig combines the worst of several worlds: the worst available profile shape, plus a complex system of support wires generating high parasitic drag, plus a fixed mast that spoils the flow of air in front of the mainsail. It can literally be said that an airplane wing with all these defects would never get off the ground.

Having said all that, let us also remind ourselves to be careful about the enthusiasm with which we directly apply aerodynamic facts to sailboats. Airplane wings are used to provide upward lift—not forward drive. And airplane wings are powered by engines at high speeds, while sails have to be their own engines—at relatively low speeds. Lots of similarities, but also some fundamental differences.

For example, if you were to rig a modern IOR hull with a clean rotating wing mast and a single full-battened elliptical sail, you would have a rig of very respectable theoretical aerodynamic efficiency. But somebody would probably beat you around the course with a boat having a very thin, highly stayed bendy mast, a bewildering array of sail options, and the knowledge of how to shift gears to match the rig to the wind conditions. The answer here is that at the pitifully low speeds achieved by even the most modern displacement hulls (six to twelve miles per hour), air drag is not nearly as significant a factor as it is in airplanes. With sailboats you have a high-drag rig lugging what amounts to a streamlined lead mine—an aggregate of defects so formidable that breakthrough speeds are out of the question. With current displacement designs we are trapped in a basically insoluble riddle—you need a heavy keel to balance the tall rig that you need to drive a heavy keel! This is a revolving door approach to forward speed, with about as much chance for success as the analogy implies.

"Well," you say, "just put on a tiny rig, and then you will only need a tiny keel or no keel." Wrong. The hull—or platform that you need to carry the people—is also a substantial drag force. So you need at least a medium rig to get a decent-sized hull moving. And without a ballasted keel, if you aren't really careful, an unexpected gust will have the bad grace to tip you over, and while this can be fun on a Sunfish it is chaos on a larger boat with bunks, galleys, cabinets, booze, etc. So there we are, back to the need for a hull ballasted by a keel, which shuts down the speed possibilities, needs a tall rig, etc., etc.

The multihulls have of course found a way out of this riddle, and can open up their speed potential accordingly. There are however some clouds on that particular horizon, which will be discussed in a separate chapter.

But before we give up on monohulls, let's probe a bit more into the nature of the drive forces available to us in the upper fluid.

FOUR

The Flow of the Upper Fluid

We have to begin with some basics. In the most common explanation of why a sailboat can sail against the wind, one invokes a comparison with the airplane wing. Everybody has come to accept, if not comprehend, that airplane wings are capable of lifting immense weights off the ground when pushed at sufficient speeds. And so, OK, it is plausible that a sail which crudely resembles the wing could generate forces capable of moving a hull against the wind. But wait a minute. The lift on an airplane wing is up, so if this same kind of force exists on a sailboat wing why doesn't it just push or suck us directly to leeward?

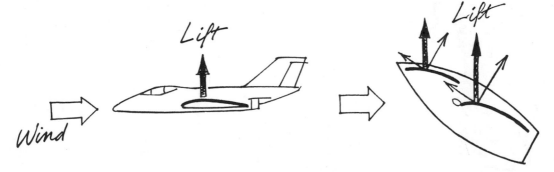

All right—sailing to windward, most of the lift forces on a sail *are* to leeward. That's why the first thing a boat does is heel when the wind hits. But there is a forward force generated, though it comes as a resultant of forces in other directions. Lift operates at approximate right angles to the sail. And because the boat's hull, keel (or centerboard), and rudder are designed to resist sideward motion more than forward motion, forward motion is extracted from the predominantly sideward force of the wind.

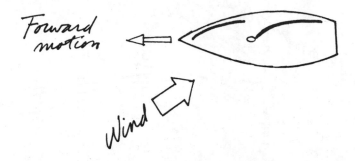

A frequent explanation of this is again based on the airplane wing. The air passing over the curved upper surface, we are told, travels a greater distance, and must therefore go faster than the air traveling the shorter distance on the bottom of the wing. So the difference in the velocities of the upper and lower air creates lower pressure on the upper side of the wing, which sucks the wing upward.

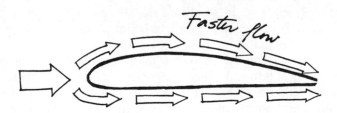

Okay, but how does that explanation hold true for a sail, which is as thin as a piece of Dacron cloth? You mean to tell me the air on one side of this cloth has an appreciably greater distance to travel than on the other?

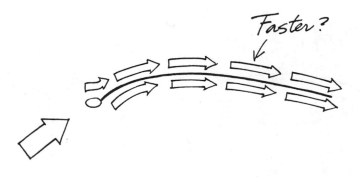

A more logical layman's explanation is that the curved sail bends or deflects the wind away from its mainstream course.

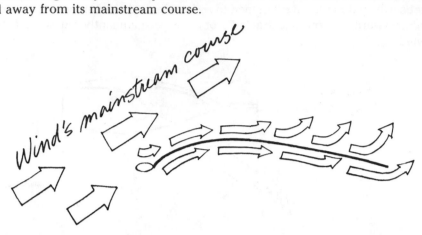

The wind on the leeward side of the sail is "pulling" to get back to mainstream course and the wind on the windward side is "pushing" to get back to mainstream course. These are the forces that conspire mysteriously to move the sailboat into a wind blowing the other way. If you overtrim, you detach the flow and lose the lift.

It is worthy of note, without torturing you with the explanation, that the wind on the leeward side of the sail is worth more—it contributes about 75 percent of the drive, versus 25 percent from the windward side. If I could give you a clear, simple account of why this is true, I would. You will be better off just accepting it in the same spirit that one concedes that $2 + 2 = 4$.

The differences between the windward performances of various rigs deserve comment. In theoretical terms, the single sail or cat rig should be the most efficient. And the boats that hold the speed records are cat-rigged, so it's not just theory. But you have to be careful about confusing flat-out speed for a highly speedy object (iceboat, catamaran, sailboard) with success on the conventional race course by a conventional, low-speed boat.

Virtually all conventional boats—even light dinghies—operate in the displacement mode to windward. Which is to say that their speed ranges from 3 knots to 8 knots, or dead slow to slow. At this tortoise pace, the ability to point becomes a highly critical factor.

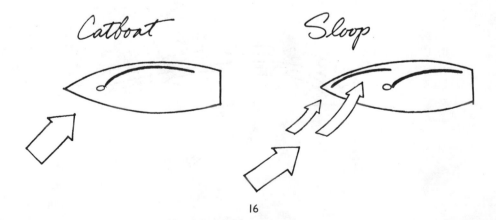

And here is where the sloop shines. The wind coming at a sail senses the object ahead of it and swerves slightly before it gets there. The mast, being the principal object in the wind's way, is the primary inducer of this deflection effect. This means that a clean-edged sail operating in front of a mast "sees" a better wind angle than it ever would as a single sail. This better wind angle enables the jib boat to consistently outpoint the catboat. Since on normal race courses about two-thirds of the time is spent sailing to windward, superior pointing ability makes the sloop rig the winner of most races. Perhaps the chief factor in pointing ability is a tight forestay on which to hang the jib; hence all the attention to backstay tension, hydraulics, etc.

The jib has the further benefit of helping to clean up the turbulent air created by the mast at the leading edge of the main. The slot effect really amounts to this—channeling air through and forcing the air flow to stay attached where it might otherwise detach. In a nice synergistic exchange, the jib makes the main work better, and the main makes the jib more efficient.

For purposes of this book, that's about all we need to know about lift in the upper fluid. C.A. Marchaj has probably the best definitive book on this subject (*The Aero-Hydrodynamics of Sailing*, Dodd, Mead, 1979), and if you need more of a sail trimmer's orientation North Sails has a very instructive booklet titled "The Fast Course Book."

Now, it does not do to be deterred or in any way overwhelmed by all this science and pseudoscience. Trying to follow all the sailing theories available will lose you more in confusion than you can possibly gain in practical application. Learned professors from learned universities might dispute this, but I have been beating learned professors around the course for years.

What we are interested in here is observable effects, and one of the first of these is that a sailboat will drive to windward, and that its drive to windward is directly enhanced by the degree to which heeling is resisted. Hike out, spill wind, reduce sail —but by all means hold your boat flat, because the sailor who holds his boat flat goes faster and points higher to windward. Part of this has to do with presenting a better hull shape in the upright mode, as well as preserving more lateral resistance via the vertical keel and rudder versus the inclined keel or rudder. But also—although it is largely unexplored—there is a clear *downward* component to the lift force that grows as the boat heels, because the lift force operates at right angles to the sail. The downward force tends to press the boat further down in the water the more it heels, and there is no way that can help forward progress. The French skipper of one of the most successful oceangoing multihulls is reported to have assessed this force on his boat as one ton of pressure downward on the leeward hull at 15 knots. Monohulls frequently operate at much greater angles of heel, so you get some idea of the negative force involved.

Maybe the best way to understand this is to observe the opposite effect when a rig is heeled to windward. Rock a windsurfer rig to windward and you will immediately feel the upward pull—the upward lift of the windward inclined sail—and yet the forward driving force is still there. As various speed trials around the world have dramatically demonstrated in recent years, it is this ability to convert the wind's force to *upward* as well as *forward* lift that enables the windsurfer literally to pull itself out of the water, reducing wetted surface so that it can "fly" ever faster. In one of the newer sail versions presented at the English speed trials (Portland Speed Week, held each year), a wing sail section is pivoted on a vertical mast, inclining from the vertical to the horizontal as the wind increases. This rig has intriguing possibilities and serves easily to illustrate several key points.

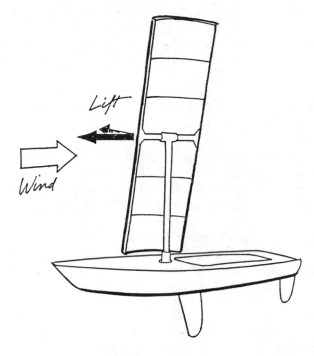

Without claiming to be scientifically precise, we could say that with such a rig in the horizontal mode the lift is almost all upward, and little forward.

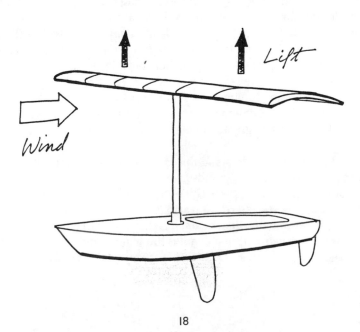

In the vertical mode, the lift force is sidewards and forward. The more you incline this rig toward the horizontal, the more upward lift, the less forward lift, and the less heeling moment are generated.

On a conventional boat heeled to leeward, the lift force is forward, sidewards, and down, and the weight and leverage of the rig to leeward is pulling the boat down more the more it heels. That's why boats that are sailed flat sail faster—they suffer less downward force.

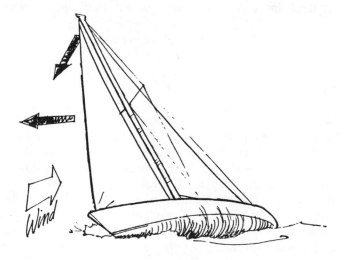

On a sailboard heeled to windward the lift force is upward and forward. Plus, the weight of the rig to windward helps counteract heeling. While the forward drive may be somewhat lessened, the downward force has been removed, and the upward lift generated creates a more easily driven object.

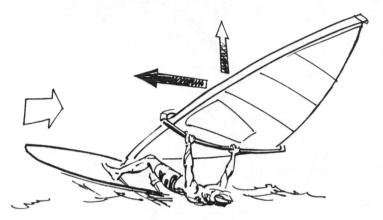

At about this point, the establishment designers will snort derisively and say "fine —but it won't work on big boats." They will try to shift your attention to elliptical keels and wing keels, and will begin Gregorian chants about prismatic coefficients and sail area–to-displacement ratios. Dismiss these ploys as diversionary tactics that may at best net a quarter knot more speed and will only lead once again down the garden path where tall rigs need heavy keels, which need tall rigs, etc.

A twelve-meter with 25 tons of lead in its keel, heeled at forty-five degrees, has managed the curious feat of optimizing the negative elements of extreme weight and downward lift while simultaneously going to extravagant lengths to concentrate on relatively minor refinements of sail shape and hull configuration that might fool the rule. From the point of view of design progress, this is elaborate pursuit of diminishing returns.

Let's reassess. If the first stage of sailing (square-riggers) was learning how to angle in front of the push of the wind, and the second stage (sloops) has been to learn how to angle more effectively into the wind, then the third stage must be learning how to harness upward lift and link it to forward drive. Because the minute we can do this, we convert a negative heeling force that had to be counteracted into a positive balancing force that heels the boat less while simultaneously lightening it by lifting it upward. The philosophy of a vertical rig to which we add lead to resist heeling only guarantees sinkability and a low speed ceiling—so that has to be a dumb solution. Adding lead is a tactic used to make race horses slower, and if you don't believe this is true, try tying ten pounds of lead around your waist and running around the block. Putting people on trapezes or hulls out to windward is also a fairly primitive solution, because it in no way harvests the positive upward lift force that the wind clearly makes available. Rather, all that hiking on trapezes or extra hulls can do is to control and thereby somewhat diminish the negative factor of heeling and its subsequent downward force. Why accept a negative force when a positive vector is available?

Clipper ships, because they couldn't go to windward, gave way to tightly stayed sloops that could. Now tightly stayed, vertically rigged sloops must give way to new solutions, because they are trapped in an unsatisfactory slow-speed syndrome.

Rigs that harness upward and forward lift will open up new hull possibilities that can free us from this slow-speed syndrome. New rigs can liberate sailing from hull and keel types whose chief reason for being is the way they control the negative forces generated by the high heeling moment and low aerodynamic efficiency of the tall, triangular, stayed sloop rig.

FIVE

Multihulls

*T*he foregoing discussion might sound like at least a partial argument for catamarans and trimarans with wing masts. If you have never sailed a multihull, give yourself a treat. Jump on a Hobie or any one of the modern catamarans and blast off the beach in the kind of speed surge you just never feel in conventional monohulls. A puff hits and you immediately accelerate, to speeds that can reach over twenty miles per hour. The boat is stable, can be sailed in shallow water right up to the beach, and it is so light you can handle it with relative ease and get those great speeds with a smaller rig.

In the larger multihulls, the Europeans have shown the way with exciting boats that now hold all the major ocean speed records. Unless the race happens to be entirely to windward, there is simply no way a displacement monohull can come close to them. But it isn't all peaches and cream with multihulls because they face some persistent practical difficulties:

1. They have great initial stability, but no ultimate stability, so they will tip over, and once they do they become extremely stable in the upside down position. This risk may be acceptable for small boats and for professional racing of larger craft for high-speed rewards—but for general use? In today's litigious society, sending people to sea on a product which by design readily tips over would take a very brave insurance company—and these don't exist anymore.

2. The wide beam that provides the stability and thereby allows the lightness creates a serious space problem at docks and marinas. Marinas either can't fit

multihulls into existing slips, or they will charge you double—which is no joke in terms of added expense.

3. The cost of producing two or three hulls and properly connecting them is as much or more than a regular boat, and the strains are such that structural failure is more likely. So construction standards for multihulls are not nearly as forgiving as they are for monohulls. Again, legal and warranty problems loom.

4. The bridge deck on a catamaran has to be at least three feet off the water to avoid slamming into waves. A center cabin placed on top of that bridge must have an additional six feet for standing headroom. That makes nine feet over the water, and to gracefully support a cabin nine feet off the water you need a hull about fifty feet long. That's tough on the thirty-foot size range that offers the biggest current sales volume. Trimarans are better in this regard, because their center hull can accommodate people and facilities in the normal manner. But cruising facilities take weight and you have to be very conscious of weight with all multihulls lest you lose the speed advantage that was the whole purpose for the exercise. Heavy multihulls are neither fast, safe, nor pretty.

Because of these problems, no large (over thirty feet) multihull has ever made it as a popular production model. I do not suggest that these difficulties are insurmountable, but they are sobering. Here again I believe that new rigs could provide the breakthrough. Modern multihulls have improved on the conventional stayed sloop rig by the use of fully battened sails and wing masts. By so doing they have moved from the demonstrated inefficiency of the triangular sail toward the more optimum elliptical shape. Wing masts have also significantly reduced the leading edge turbulence of the mast that cripples conventional mainsails. So the benefits are there, but they are not troublefree. Wing masts are cumbersome, expensive, and difficult to de-power at rest. To be fully effective the wing mast needs to be carried at an angle closer to the wind than the rest of the sail. This involves separate adjustment controls for the wing mast, and these can get complex. At anchor or at a dock the wing is an aerodynamic force that can make the boat want to go just when you want it to sit still.

No account of catamaran speed would be complete without mention of the C-Class cats (so-rated by the International Yacht Racing Union) that blaze around the course in pursuit of the "Little America's Cup" (the International Catamaran Challenge Trophy, held annually). It is a pity the sailing world doesn't pay more attention to these remarkable craft and the small group of brilliant engineers who produce them. Using slotted wing spars, these C-Cats are capable of dramatic speeds, and they regularly outpace the wind. These wing masts are technological wonders which by contrast point up the gross inefficiency of conventional rigs. But while marveling at its ingenuity, it is hard to bring this branch of sailing technology down to practical levels, because it requires complexity—a knowledge of complexity, and even a love of complexity.

Critically, none of the multihull rigs have yet taken advantage of the upward lifting force of the wind that is there for the asking. By blindly sticking to the vertical sloop rig, in most cases they have locked themselves into accepting the full heeling force that is the first cause of their most prominent failing—tipping over. Multihulls would clearly profit from a rig that would reduce the heeling moment of the wind and convert part of that force to a balancing upward lift. This would relieve pressure on the leeward hull, making multihulls significantly faster and safer. Multihulls have taken the smart step of shedding lead, but they somewhat compromised that gain by sacrificing ultimate stability. *New rigs that offer better stability would thus directly enhance multihull appeal by minimizing their primary sales defect.*

SIX

Streamlining as a New Key

My experiments with pedal-powered boats have been most instructive in this area. Streamlining was critical there, because even the strongest muscles in the human body (the legs) make such a puny engine (about one-half horsepower) that great care has to be taken to minimize the restraining factors. The need for underwater efficiency in boats is obvious, and everybody understands why you need a smooth, slippery underwater shape. But air drag is almost equally important, though much less well attended.

Consider that when an Olympic bicyclist pumps at top speed (about 32 miles per hour), nine out of every ten pumps go just to push air out of the way. When the cyclist is inclined to a horizontal posture and enclosed in a streamlined capsule, he can pedal 58 miles per hour! That's almost twice the speed with the same horsepower, and underscores the exciting improvements that can be had by rearranging the same elements in different form.

The accompanying photographs show the Waterbug and the Mallard, two streamlined, pedal-powered propeller boats I have designed. I use these to illustrate how better results can be obtained from the same source of energy. Given the problem of a "human" engine with its previously stated low horsepower, it becomes clear with study that the most popular methods of propulsion (rowing and paddling) are not the most efficient utilization of the energy available. Rowing and paddling fail on four counts:

1. They do not use the strongest muscles of the body—the legs. (Shells with sliding seats do—but not primarily.)

25

The highly streamlined bullet shape of the Waterbug enables a person to slip through wind and wave with minimum effort. This boat can be pedaled upwind in 40 knots with relative ease.

These photos of the Mallard-model pedal/prop boat show the benefits of streamlining. The aerodynamic nose cleanly sheds a wall of water, enabling the boat to handle waves that would swamp a conventional dinghy. Air, being a fluid, will flow around the nose in a similar fashion.

2. The power is necessarily intermittent, because the recovery strokes don't count for forward propulsion.

3. The action of rowing or paddling requires an open boat, which prohibits an enclosed, streamlined shape.

4. The process of propulsion requires an exposed human torso and arms, plus oars or paddles. In a strong headwind these non-aerodynamic surfaces create almost as much windage and backward drag as the oars and paddles can generate forward power.

By way of improvement, both the Waterbug and Mallard:

1. use the strongest muscles in the body (leg drive with back braced);

2. create constant power by linking rotary leg motion to a propeller;

3. utilize a streamlined shape to minimize drag; and

4. recline the human body for smaller frontal shape and no exposed surfaces.

By way of payoff, you can pedal the Waterbug with no difficulty when it's blowing over 40 knots, conditions in which a shell, kayak, or rowed dinghy—or even an outboard inflatable—would be totally unmanageable. The photo of the Mallard bursting through surf shows how its streamlined shape cleanly sheds the water and simultaneously provides the driver with protection, allowing performance that a non-streamlined shape could not hope to match.

How does this relate to sailing? Applying the same analysis to the average stayed sloop, we find:

1. The rig does not use the available power in the most efficient manner, because the profile shape is wrong, mast and rigging create turbulence and drag, and the negative penalty of heeling force is accepted.

2. The nature of sail operation requires an open deck with lifelines and exposed crew. Deck streamlining is prohibited by the traditional system of handling sails.

As photographs of the Delta 26 (Chapter 10) show, it is demonstrably possible to have a sailboat with an aerodynamic nose. The trick is to design sail handling and anchoring systems that can be handled from the cockpit. Isn't that better than servile acceptance of the status quo?

The thrust of this brief chapter is to show that preconceived notions of what sailboat hulls, decks, and rigs should be have the detrimental effect of blocking out the highly desirable advantages of streamlining. Streamlining could make sailboats shed both air and water better, which would mean safer, faster, drier boats. Why should we accept sailboat shapes that are flagrant aerodynamic failures when design ingenuity can harness the same source of energy in different ways—ways that will improve the drive and reduce the drag?

SEVEN

The 50-Knot Sailboat

*T*he present record of 36+ knots is held by *Crossbow*, an English proa multihull especially designed for speed trials. Close behind, and closing fast at 35+ knots, are various boardsailors on much smaller but equally fast boats. It is clear that 40 knots is well within reach, and should be attained in the near future. Since 40 knots is, for practical purposes, already done, I have turned my thoughts to the next hurdle of 50 knots. I deliberately place the bar 10 knots higher in order to encourage completely fresh thinking, rather than just a refinement of the boats currently closing in on 40 knots. Obviously any boat that breaks 40 knots can—with careful polishing—be made to do 41 knots. So let's aim here for a bigger jump.

I believe our first efforts should concentrate on the rig. After all, the rig is the drive force, while the hull is essentially a drag force. The trick is to maximize the former and minimize the latter. Minimize is a good word, for the boardsailors have shown that smaller can indeed be better, and they are now setting their speed records on what amount to water skis that are far simpler and less expensive than the large multihulls that also aspire to the records.

It is well to recall that when man set out to reach the moon, the pessimists began recounting all the reasons it couldn't be done. They pointed out that there were no engines available with the necessary force, no metals available capable of withstanding the heat, and no navigation systems available to find the target and return. As was quickly proven, those were not reasons why the job couldn't be done—they were merely reasons why it had not been done before.

Our target of 50 knots is of course ridiculously modest alongside the scope of the moon effort. But let's lay out the things we first need in the rig:

1. A foil profile shape of maximum efficiency in order to minimize induced drag.

2. A camber shape and texture capable of maximizing lift and drive.

3. The ability to create upward lift as well as forward drive.

4. Exposed surfaces must all be aerodynamic.

5. The ability to handle extremely high winds.

It goes without saying that these criteria completely disqualify existing stayed sloop rigs. They just don't make it on any of these counts, *which is a sad comment on the state of the art.* The modern sailboard rigs are indeed the best in the field, but they begin to fall down on points four and five. Neither the wishbone boom nor the operator is very aerodynamic on sailboards. Since the operator is necessary to hold up the rig, he must be considered part of the rig, and on a sailboard he represents probably sixty percent of the drag. Also, while boardsailors have handled and set their records in high winds, the size of the rig is definitely limited by what human strength can hold up. Limiting the rig's horsepower is not a likely way to get us over the 50-knot hump.

In terms of better drive efficiency, one is immediately attracted to rigid foils. After all, the firmer you make the shape, and the smoother the surface texture, the better the "sail" efficiency. Modern racing sails come very close to being sheets of plastic, so why not go the next step and make our 50-knot sails out of curved sheets of plastic or aluminum? The problem with rigid foils has always been their unmanageability. A rigid foil of the high aspect ratio necessary to be efficient must be very tall and narrow. Cross this with the minimum sail area needed to power the craft (three hundred square feet or so) and you have a foil that must be at least thirty feet high. That's already tough to handle, and if we have a set curve to the foil, the boat only goes on one tack. Well, *Crossbow*, the current record holder, only goes on one tack, so that's not necessarily a disqualifying negative—but it undeniably makes an awkward arrangement.

The balanced rotating wing described earlier is one way around this.

This ingenious rig allows you to de-power the sail in the horizontal mode, which means you can put the rig in neutral and wait on the beach or on the dock without having the whole works sail away. And it enables you to adjust to increasing winds simply by inclining the rig away from the vertical toward the horizontal, thus exchanging damaging heeling moment for useful upward lift. Not bad—in fact, damn good, because it begins to meet the challenge of converting heeling moment to lift.

The trouble is, this high-aspect-ratio wing still has to be about thirty feet long to get us the necessary minimum three hundred square feet, and that's still a rather unmanageable object. Moreover, we have to support that wing on a strong structure and add control lines and wires, none of which can be productive in an aerodynamic sense because they are all pure drag.

My solution to this dilemma is the Circular Linked Foil Rig. Instead of settling for a single foil, this arrangement stacks a number of foils like curved slats within a circular duct.

As can be seen by the sketch, the circular linked foil is mounted like a propeller forward of an aerodynamic rotating pylon, which supports it. The angle this circular linked foil makes to the wind is controlled by rotating the pylon. The desired conver-

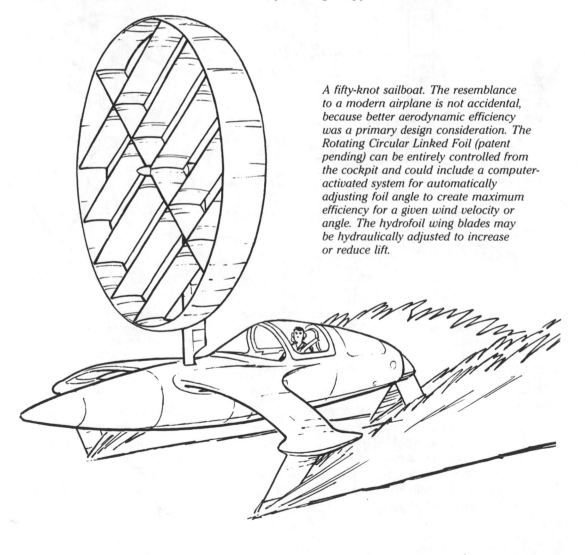

A fifty-knot sailboat. The resemblance to a modern airplane is not accidental, because better aerodynamic efficiency was a primary design consideration. The Rotating Circular Linked Foil (patent pending) can be entirely controlled from the cockpit and could include a computer-activated system for automatically adjusting foil angle to create maximum efficiency for a given wind velocity or angle. The hydrofoil wing blades may be hydraulically adjusted to increase or reduce lift.

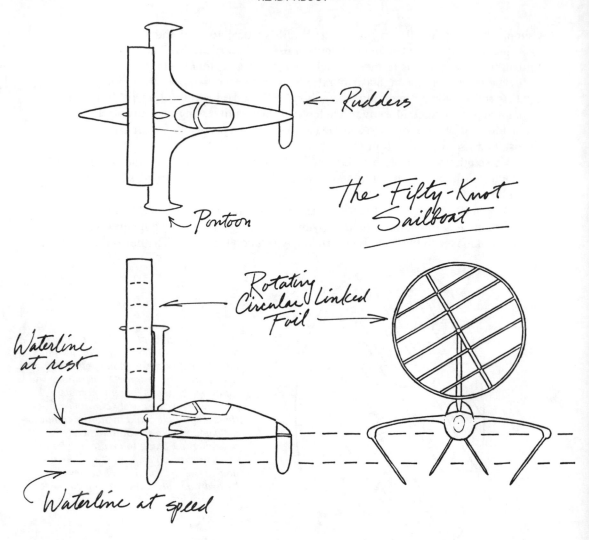

The front view here best shows the multiple, thin aerodynamic sections that this rig presents to the wind. Being extremely light and low, the Circular Linked Foil experiences far less heeling moment than conventional rigs, and its balanced nature can readily convert wasted heeling force into useful upward lift.

sion of heeling moment to lift is accomplished by rotating the wheel around the propeller hub, so that the parallel foils move from the vertical toward the horizontal. Since the loads are balanced and the whole rig turns on the center hub, this rotation is mechanically easy and may be accomplished by means contained within the streamlined pylon. Both controls—the rotating of the pylon (trim) and the rotating of the circular foil (heel control and lift conversion)—can be managed by one operator from within a streamlined compartment, with no external wires or lines.

It can be seen that this rig does three very desirable things:

1. It provides efficient high-aspect-ratio foils without the penalty of great height, which equates to high heeling moment. The necessary sail area is gained by the simple expedient of stacking a number of smaller high-aspect foils sideways instead of pushing one large foil up.

2. By containing these smaller high-aspect-ratio foils within a circular duct, we harmoniously channel the incoming wind and provide the foils a beneficial end-plate effect that improves lift.

3. By rotating the wheel around a center hub we obtain a balanced mechanism that can be easily controlled without the need for cumbersome ropes or wires.

Stop for a moment and think how far this rig takes us from the frustrating riddle in which a tall rig needs a heavy keel to hold it, which needs a tall rig to drive it, etc., etc.

As stated, stacking the foils enables us to lower the rig dramatically, thus substantially reducing the heeling moment, which in turn reduces and simplifies our hull balance requirements. Spacing sails horizontally has been tried before—most notably by an English design, which had some five sails mounted horizontally on a multihull. This rig achieved some interesting success, but it was hampered by its basic ungainliness. After all, that's a lot of trouble to go to when one man on an eight-pound board can go faster! The Circular Linked Foil Rig takes an important step forward. Containing and mounting the foils in a circular duct has the happy virtue of creating a very rigid structure that enables all the parts to be very thin and light, features which directly enhance their aerodynamic contribution as well. And the circle, being the most balanced design available, enables the whole thing to be extremely compact and easily rotated.

Note that it would also be possible to directly utilize a human operator to rotate this linked circular foil on what could be a very fast board boat. This might be the most economical approach to the 50-knot barrier, but a larger craft could reach more exciting speeds because of better drag control and more horsepower.

A human operator could rotate the linked circular foil on a board boat with good results, though a larger boat could achieve more exciting speeds. On the sailboard, where light weight is critical, the walls of the duct are replaced by two rails, sacrificing the end-plate effect for a saving in weight and ease of holding.

Critics will be quick to see that this Circular Linked Foil Rig won't do much directly downwind—a course for which conventional hulls must add sail area. The answer is that the rig requires a speedy hull—like iceboats, catamarans, or boards—so that it is always going fast enough never to be going dead downwind. (If you go fast enough, you make your own wind, and are in effect always sheeting in.) So to properly complement this rig, we have to look at faster hulls.

A trip to the 1986 London Boat Show revealed to me a hull/foil configuration of great promise. This boat, called "The Hydrofoil Sailing Boat," was designed by Miles Handley and utilizes hydrofoils in a somewhat different and very interesting manner. Again, it is not totally new, but to see their tape of this boat slipping along at high speed with absolutely minimal fuss is very convincing. When it's going, there are only four thin blades in the water—the faster you go, the less blade. And, while I have previously termed the hull as simply a drag force, these very effective angled foils obviously contribute a positive lift force as well. This seems like a real step forward, a lot better than the many overly complex foil contraptions. There may be problems controlling those freestanding foil tips, but modern materials such as carbon fiber can deliver amazing stiffness with low weight.

Designer Handley and his group are themselves very committed to breaking the 40-knot barrier, and I would rate their chances as excellent. Unfortunately, their present rig does not live up to the sophistication of their foils. It is really nothing more than a large sailboard sail, and not a very modern one at that.

I would recommend adapting my Circular Linked Foil Rig to some version of a foil hull. In this way we would achieve the desirable combination of a rig that extracts lift and drive from the upper medium with a hull that extracts lift from the lower medium. Contrast that with present rigs that deliver no lift, placed on hulls that deliver no lift.

I would estimate that with a budget of $200,000 and one year's time to develop a prototype, the 40-knot goal could be assured, and the 50-knot goal seriously assaulted. Some $300,000 and two years would get you 50 knots.

Of course, this expenditure is laughably low compared to the dollars spent annually on IOR freaks and twelve-meter stegosaurs. It is ironic that one maxi-boat contender is currently spending *more on the tank test models* to develop a design that might yield a possible one knot advantage on a hull that cannot exceed fourteen knots than he would need to spend to obtain the actual boat that could exceed 50 knots. That seems amazingly disoriented when we're talking about "race" boats.

The attainment of these exciting higher velocities would vault sailing out of its present horse-and-buggy image into the realm of speed objects which the public clearly fancies. The wider public interest that is automatically assured by these new speed capacities would begin to make the sport more attractive to commercial sponsors. Commercial sponsors mean more seed money, which would automatically attract brighter minds to work on the problems and opportunities. This would create steady progress in place of the devious detours that currently characterize sailboat design efforts.

It also doesn't take too much imagination to see that a fuel-free water vehicle capable of 50-knot speeds could in some regions begin to have useful commercial value. If only to deliver mail or medicines between islands or along coasts where

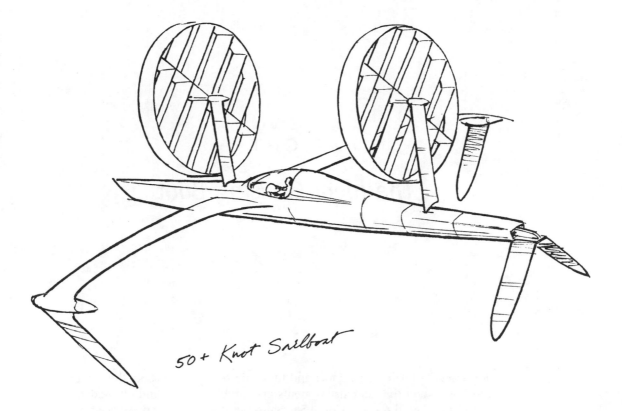

50 + Knot Sailboat

This larger and swifter version shows "double engine" use of the Circular Linked Foils. The advantage here is that sail area is doubled, but the center of effort stays very low, enabling this rig to handle the extremely high winds that will be necessary to generate 50+ knots. A dashboard of instruments will monitor performance for the pilot, and the balance of the craft will be controlled by computers automatically adjusting the angle of the foils to counter changes in wind velocity.

strong, steady winds prevail, it could nonetheless serve as a stimulating reactivation of commercial sail power. The Circular Linked Foil Rig of course lends itself to plastic or aluminum construction, giving it high durability and low maintenance compared to cloth sails, which literally shake themselves to death.

There might even be some military feasibility. Considering the billions of dollars the U.S. has spent to develop a Stealth bomber, whose all plastic body is supposed to make it radar invisible, maybe we would be better off with a lot of silent, all plastic, speed sailboats. Hell, if we could just grab part of the Defense Department's budget for $8,000 coffee makers, we could work wonders!

The attainment of more sailing speed is a tangible, practical goal, but only worth trying if the speed levels can come up to what is perceived by the public to be exciting levels. Ten miles per hour doesn't make it. The sooner we can get competitive sailing's focus off the frivolous pursuit of minor gain for major costs and into the realm of real speeds, the better off the sport will be.

EIGHT

The Ideal Cruising Boat

*L*et's slow down a bit from 50 knots and futuristic designs. I suspect the foregoing gives the impression that all existing boats are hopelessly dull and outmoded. Not true for cruising. Yes, there are a lot of Sea Slugs out there whose appeal is a mystery to me, but there are also a lot of men very happy with women out there whose charm completely escapes me. The fact is that standards for cruising boats are extremely relaxed, to the point that performance standards are almost meaningless.

This observation runs counter to the current promotion of "performance cruising," hype in which I have participated. It has taken me awhile to realize that relaxation is the first reason for, and benefit of, cruising. Once that is clear, it is obvious that performance, while a factor, is extremely secondary to the cruiser—well behind comfort and security as a buying concern. If you require practical evidence of this, remember that the best-selling cruising design of all time is the Morgan Out Island 41. No one has ever accused this design of stellar performance; in fact its inability to go to windward is legendary. In the prototype Freedom 40, I can recall literally sailing circles around a Morgan 41 that was plodding along at its customary tortoise pace. But getting down to sales figures, we discover that the Morgan Out Island 41 out-performs everybody, with a record of over 1200 units sold. Nobody comes even close to that sales figure in that size range. And since sales are the best measuring tool we have for popularity, the inescapable conclusion is that, for the cruiser, other things come ahead of performance.

This means that displacement hulls with lead keels (a concept that makes no performance sense) are likely to be around for a long time on the cruising scene, because they deliver the primary benefits of relaxation, comfort, security, and load-carrying capacity.

The heated debate between the merits of full-length keels versus fin keels is painful evidence of the cruising division's unerring instinct for stoutly resisting the obvious while zeroing closely in on the inconsequential. The full-length keel so admired by many cruisers came about not so much as a conscious design choice for a preferred seaworthy shape, but rather as a reflection of the practical limitations of planked wood construction. When all boats were made by nailing or screwing planks to frames, these planks were of course prone to leak at the seams, and anything tending to twist the planks open was a serious risk to be avoided at any cost. The prospect of hanging a heavy weight at the unsupported end of a narrow fin (clearly the best choice for hydrodynamic lift) was a shipwright's nightmare calculated to lever open the tightest seam, and so that option was justifiably rejected in favor of enclosing the lead ballast within a long, planked hull. The resulting long, enclosed keels had the further advantage of allowing fishermen to run their boats in at high tide and then work on them at low tide, a convenience which the fin keel virtually prohibits. Great for 1930.

But the single-shell strength of fiberglass totally eliminated the seam leakage consideration, and made suspending a fin a relatively simple construction problem. More modern methods of hauling made grounding boats a thing of the past, so the two prime negatives against fin keels were removed. As the classic Cal 40 quickly proved about 40 years ago, a canoe shape with a fin keel would develop less leeward slip than a full-length keel of the same depth, and the considerable reduction of wetted surface made the hull much more easily driven. So sailboats with fin keels required less sail area for equal speed, and could, as a bonus, be induced to surf in front of large waves in a strong wind. In terms of speed performance there was no contest, since the fin keel promptly wiped out the full-length keel both upwind and down.

Unhappily, the International Offshore Rule, with its penchant for rewarding frivolity, quickly produced a number of fin-keeled freaks whose most distinguishing characteristic was their uncanny ability to broach on a dime. Whereas the full-length keel necessarily had an attached rudder which, if unattended, wanted to steer straight, the IOR deviations would dive left or right indiscriminately at the slightest provocation. This gave the fin keel a bad name that the concept did not at all deserve. The ability to steer straight does not require a full-length keel anymore than an arrow requires a full-length feather to fly true. In fact, an arrow with a full-length feather will scarcely fly at all, which ought to tell you something about the efficiency of full-length keels. If the ability to let go the wheel and have the boat continue to go straight is the desired characteristic, this can be accomplished simply by hanging the rudder on a skeg behind the fin. It won't steer quite as well or as easily as a balanced rudder, but it will try to steer straight. So you can have a fin keel design that will track as true as any full-length keel yet be considerably faster, and if you want to turn sharply it will spin on the fin instead of trying to drag a long, ungainly keel around. Put a knife in the water vertically, and it spins easily. Put it in horizontally and it spins hard.

Backed into a corner by these realities, die-hard adherents of the full-length keel will usually retreat to sermons about better seakeeping qualities while hove-to under storm trysail in Force 10 winds. Since that condition is in any case off the Richter scale in terms of misery, arguments about comfort are highly relative at best. Besides, the greater speed potential of the fin keel would allow the smart sailor to be snug in harbor while the full-length keel is still wallowing in the waves. Yes, a fin keel and a spade rudder will tend to pick up more lobster pots, but these are most frequently encountered in New England waters, where most sailors' heads are so firmly encased in tradition they are not likely to look up for the next ten years anyway. Full-length keels are likely to be with us for a long time, and, like the broad-tailed ladies they resemble, God bless them.

Accepting this, areas of possible improvement are quickly reduced to the rig, because good displacement hulls and comfortable interiors are plentifully available in both present and used boats. In recent years we have seen how innovations such as furling gear gained quick and universal appeal with cruisers, because they enhance the ability to relax by reducing trouble. There is plenty of room for useful innovation in this area.

Let me use the Hoyt Gun Mount as an example. It is an observable fact that all displacement hulls share the need to add extra sail offwind to achieve their hull speed potential in light or medium winds. Cruising boats, with their heavier hulls and shorter rigs, find themselves particularly underpowered offwind. Moreover, one-half of their insufficient power is in the genoa jib, which we all know twists off and slats about downwind without contributing much except bother. The only way to add sail area effectively is with a pole and spinnaker, which spreads a lot of area and gets some of it out to windward. The so-called cruising spinnakers, those without poles, are a help reaching—but no good downwind.

The problem is that poled spinnakers are difficult and labor-intensive devices requiring the skilled knowledge of several people, and this has made them deservedly unpopular with the cruiser. Yet if a way could be found to make spinnaker power easily and safely handled by one person entirely from the cockpit, the spinnaker could earn reconsideration and become a welcome sail in the cruising inventory. So instead of a pole resting against the mast (which has to be set up, removed, and changed every time you jibe), I mounted a sliding yard on the bow pulpit. That gave a balanced rig, and the spinnaker could then be launched from and retrieved to a tube on deck. Well, it works. The Gun Mount has been in use on over 600 boats, and if you'll just ask the man who owns one, you'll find he swears by it. The Gun Mount Spinnaker was used on a Freedom 65 that stormed across the Atlantic in 13 days 10 hours, one of the faster passages ever made. With this invention anybody can hoist, jibe, and douse the spinnaker from the cockpit, and the ability to do this adds a new dimension of fun and speed to the cruising boat without the worry and hassle long associated with the spinnaker. Having the Gun Mount can make the difference between being able to continue under the pleasure of sail, versus being forced to turn on the engine because your boat is barely moving. In the newest version, soon to be on the market, I have developed a roller-furling spinnaker, which for the first time allows roller reefing of this sail. If the wind comes up, and you want a little less chute, just roll it down a bit. The best cruises are those devoid of crisis excitement. The thrills that bring smiles to the racer bring frowns to the cruiser, who aims for a different kind of sailing pleasure. That doesn't mean he enjoys sailing any less—he just wants to make sure things stay under control, and there's plenty of seamanship challenge in that.

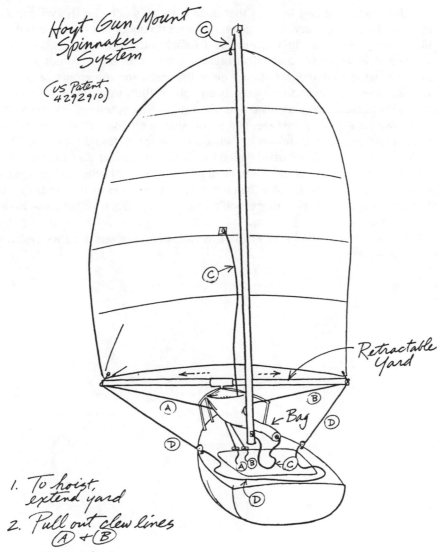

Hoyt Gun Mount
Spinnaker
System

(US Patent
4292910)

Retractable
Yard

← Bag

1. To hoist,
   extend yard
2. Pull out clew lines
   Ⓐ + Ⓑ
3. Hoist halyard Ⓒ
4. Control yard with reins Ⓓ
5. Douze by easing halyard Ⓒ
   + pulling on retrieval line Ⓒ
   (continuous line with halyard)
6. When center patch enters retrieval
   bag, ease off clew lines Ⓐ + Ⓑ
7. Spinnaker is completely stored
   in retrieval bag

In these terms, it can be seen that neither today's nor yesterday's cruisers are ever going to be out of style, and given the wide diversity of cruising purposes, it is unlikely any one ideal rig will emerge triumphant. Sloops, yawls, ketches, and schooners all have a place and will always have their cruising devotees. But appreciation for what is available should not deter the quest for something better. Sloops, yawls, ketches, and schooners have been rather thoroughly explored, and logic suggests these rigs have plateaued near the top of their potential. For dramatic new progress we must look elsewhere, and in this search we must start with open minds without any preconceived notion of "what a cruising rig should look like." We must be willing to reconsider discarded options, because new materials can make old ideas come alive again. There is room and need for new kinds of cruising boats, which by innovative design are both faster than today's racers and easier than today's cruisers. In the tradition of L. Francis Herreshoff's *Ticonderoga*, these will become classics of a newer style.

In the next few chapters we will look at various rig options and their potential for cruising improvement.

NINE

The Freedom Rig

I have a special fondness for the Freedom rig because I pioneered it and quite literally force-fed it to a skeptical yachting public. Having now sold Freedom Yachts to the excellent builder Everett Pearson, I can perhaps survey the rig more calmly and dispassionately.

No one living today can claim to have invented the freestanding (unstayed) spar, because God did that with the tree. All I did was propose that the unstayed mast, which already worked fine on Sunfish, Lasers, Finns, and various catboats, might well work on larger cruising boats as well. The fact that this rather modest proposal created such controversy and was termed "revolutionary" gives you some idea of the timidity and turgidity that currently afflicts sailing design thought.

As a Finn sailor I had learned to like sailing alone, but I found this was not easily done on conventional large cruising boats. It is quickly observable that a sail behind a mast, on a boom, with a block purchase, is far more manageable than a large jib, which must be tensioned with no mechanical advantage. So why not forget the jib and maximize the main? The freestanding spar emerged as simply a better and safer way to handle a large mainsail. When the wind blows, the freestanding spar just bends back, flattening the sail and easing the leech, which directly de-powers the sail. Modern, tightly stayed racing sloops go to great hydraulic pressures and expense to achieve mechanically what the freestanding rig does naturally. And getting rid of all the stays makes a safer rig, because you are not placing your trust in a host of potential breaking points. *That's why wires were taken off airplane wings long ago.*

The first Freedom boats (the Freedom 40 and Freedom 33) employed a two-ply wraparound sail, the idea being to improve the flow at the leading edge by having

The prototype Freedom 40 reaching at top speed off Antigua in 1976. The offwind performance of this boat was exceptional, equaling or exceeding race boats of similar size. One person could easily handle the rig in conditions like these.

the sail convert the mast to a more aerodynamic shape. This worked, but it was difficult to explain to people how to properly hoist, lower, and reef. Any wishbone sail requires that you ease the outhaul before trying to hoist or lower sail—otherwise the sail is in tension and considerable friction results, impeding any movement up or down the mast. People just didn't seem to grasp this, and the rig began to get a bum rap about being hard to hoist or lower.

This was unfortunate, because the wraparound sail had genuine virtues that somehow went unnoticed. It is a supremely reliable sail, and having no slides, grooves, or tracks removes almost all possibility of mechanical failure. There is a pleasing performance edge as well, but it seems to take a seasoned sailor to develop this rig's potential. John Oakeley—former world champion in the Flying Dutchman, Olympic sailor, and twelve-meter helmsman—now sails a Freedom 35 in England, and he has produced some remarkable wins with the wraparound sail. Former Mallory Cup winner and E-Scow champion Cliff Campbell recently sailed his Freedom 44 to cruising class victories in all four of the major Caribbean regattas— at Puerto Rico, St. Thomas, British Virgin Islands, and Antigua. And John Carson won both legs of the Bermuda One-Two Regatta in a Freedom 44 with wraparound

Like the Freedom 40, the Freedom 33 featured a two-ply wraparound sail.

sails, including a record passage of 83 hours for the return trip to Newport. So the results were there, but tuning the average sailor into them was a perplexing and ultimately discouraging puzzle.

I had long been intrigued by full-length battens, but they were not practical on the two-ply sail, because there was nothing to restrain the battens from thrusting forward. So to ease hoisting and lowering and permit the efficiency of full-length battens, the Freedom rig shifted to conventional track and slides on the masts and eliminated the wishbone boom. This gave away some efficiency at the leading edge but picked up compensating efficiency at the trailing edge, and it also allowed a bigger, better-handling, and better-setting sail.

The freestanding spar gets you out of the triangular trap formed by the mast and backstay and permits a fully curved roach on the sail. This directly improves the profile shape by getting closer to the ideal ellipse and thus reducing induced drag. And full-length battens, in conjunction with the old idea of lazyjacks, make a supremely quiet, efficient, and manageable sail that literally stacks itself on the boom like a venetian blind.

I then developed a Continuous Line Reefing System that enables one person to

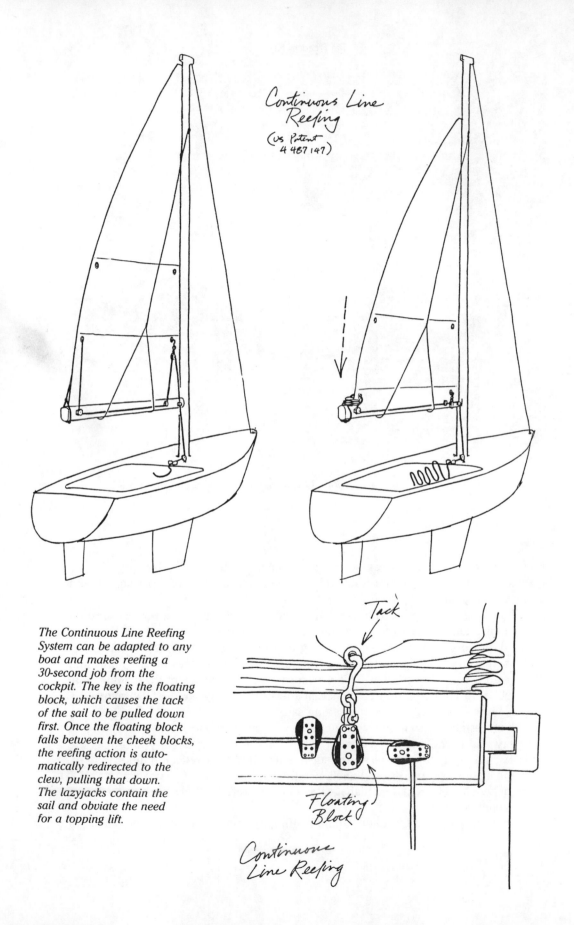

Continuous Line
Reefing
(US Patent
4 487 147)

The Continuous Line Reefing System can be adapted to any boat and makes reefing a 30-second job from the cockpit. The key is the floating block, which causes the tack of the sail to be pulled down first. Once the floating block falls between the cheek blocks, the reefing action is automatically redirected to the clew, pulling that down. The lazyjacks contain the sail and obviate the need for a topping lift.

Tack

Floating Block

Continuous
Line Reefing

reef the sail in about thirty seconds, without ever leaving the cockpit. This is significantly better than slab or jiffy reefing, a two-step process that involves more time, plus the danger of going on deck. Actually, the Continuous Line Reefing System would work on any mainsail.

Iceboats, catamarans, and sailboards have shown clearly that full-length battens make the fastest sails, and experience now shows they also make the best-behaved cruising sails. The net benefit of a freestanding spar and full-length battens is a cruising rig that is easier and safer to sail shorthanded. You simply don't need a lot of crew with this arrangement, and freeing sailors from that nuisance was the basic concept behind the Freedom program.

Are there any drawbacks? Sure. The Freedom rig is slower to windward than a sloop rig. Much easier to handle, but slightly slower, and it doesn't point as high. The rig is faster than a sloop reaching or running, but on a conventional triangular race course—where two-thirds of the time is spent to windward—the sloops win. To my way of thinking, a cruising boat that was safer, faster on a reach and a run, and easier upwind represented real progress. It still amazes me that a lot of sailors don't see that, and cling tenaciously to rigs that just can't deliver ease, safety, or simplicity, and whose only saving grace is fractional superiority to windward accompanied by pointless hard labor. Habits die hard.

Many multihull owners have inquired about the suitability of the Freedom rig for their boats. In most cases I recommend against this. On catamarans, obviously, there is an immediate problem getting enough bury in the bridge deck to support the mast. And on both catamarans and trimarans, the availability of an extremely wide staying base makes a stayed mast attractively practical. After all, it is the high compression loads on the masts of conventional yachts, occasioned by their narrow staying bases, that cause most masts to break. The wide base available on all multihulls makes staying a very simple solution and avoids the severe strains that actually distort the hulls of modern, stayed sloops.

In summary, the freestanding mast of the Freedom rig does not make a good racing solution, because it cannot be made to carry a large genoa effectively. There is simply no denying the effectiveness of a large, overlapping foresail in terms of creating more drive to windward in lighter winds and improved pointing ability in all winds. The Freedom rig, however, really comes into its own as a cruising solution, where to my mind it beats the stayed rig on almost every count. The use of a small wishbone jib on the Freedom rig—the cat sloop concept—was first introduced on the Freedom 32 and proved directly effective in better windward performance without in any way adding to difficulty of handling. Further refinements in the lightness and stiffness of carbon fiber spars will undoubtedly improve the performance of the Freedom rig, and I suspect that as a cruising solution this arrangement will steadily gain favor, because it is demonstrably safer and simpler.

I have fond moments of nostalgia recalling some of my early exploits in the prototype Freedom 40. She had no engine, and for calms employed large sweep oars just as the old fishermen did. This worked fine (as long as there was no strong tide), but I can still remember the reaction from the great unwashed public at boat shows: "Hey Martha, c'mon over here and see the slave ship—you're gonna have to row it." Needless to say, Martha was neither amused nor interested, and I was rudely awak-

*The Freedom 44 **(above)** was a refinement of the Freedom 40. This model still holds the two-handed record for the Bermuda One-Two Race with a passage of 83 hours from Bermuda to Newport. Like the 44, the Freedom 39 **(below)** has fully battened sails that stack neatly between the lazyjacks. This arrangement is hard to beat for cruising ease in terms of reefing and stowing.*

The Freedom 65 was the largest freestanding-sparred sailing yacht ever built. Its wraparound sails were difficult to handle—fully battened sails would have been easier. Nonetheless, this boat —with a skilled crew under skipper Rob James—made an Atlantic crossing (west to east) of 13 days 10 hours, demonstrating the potential for this rig. Her carbon fiber masts were stronger than solid aluminum of the same diameter.

This illustration of the Freedom 32 shows the Hoyt Gun Mount spinnaker, a fully battened mainsail, and the Continuous Line Reefing System, all having the same objective—ease and efficiency for the cruising sailor.

ened to the reality that nobody comes between the American cruiser and his love for the internal combustion engine.

Nonetheless, sailing that Freedom 40 for two and a half years without an engine did make me a seaman, where I was formerly just a racer. I sailed singlehanded in and out of most of the major harbors of the Caribbean, always in tight quarters and usually right up to the dock. The cat ketch with two equal sails is nifty for this, because you can actually steer with the sails. With this rig and a good dinghy to row out lines and anchors, one can literally sail in and out of anywhere. Okay—I'll admit an engine is easier, but we have managed to breed a generation of sailors who are either afraid or don't know how to sail in and out of harbor. Without worshipping hardship for its own sake, it still seems a good idea to know your boat well enough that the engine becomes a convenience, not a necessity. But I don't expect to win that argument, and in making it I may be guilty of the same kind of macho bravado that keeps alienating people from sail.

TEN

The Delta Rig

There are only three basic available positions for the mast:

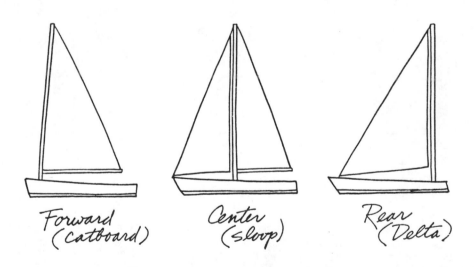

Forward
(catboard)

Center
(sloop)

Rear
(Delta)

Since I had already explored the catboat and cat ketch with the Freedom rig, and the sloop has been done ad nauseum—what about the delta? This idea is not new: Phil Bolger, the innovative small-boat designer, reports having seen it over fifty years ago. So it has been done, and from a theoretical point of view the wind doesn't much care where you put the mast so long as you keep the center of sail effort roughly over the center of lateral resistance.

There are some immediate advantages to having the mast in the rear. We have seen that putting the mast in front of a sail reduces the sail's efficiency by creating turbulence at the vital leading edge, spoiling the air flow. Neither the catboat nor the sloop can get away from that, but the delta rig can. So right away we get one or two sails with completely clean leading edges. That has to be better.

Second, a little analysis reveals that the rearward incline of the sail area gives us some upward lift off the wind. To prove this to yourself, observe how closely this rig resembles a sailboard on a reach. Anytime you rake a mast or sail aft and then let out the sail, you have created an inclined wing with an upward lift force.

And third, the windage of mast and stays in the rear tries to head the boat up into the wind, while a mast placed forward or in the middle tends to blow the bow away from the wind. This means that the delta rig behaves beautifully at anchor or on a mooring, much better than a catboat or sloop, both of which try to sail around in an often disconcerting manner.

Not content with theory, I went ahead and designed and built the prototype Delta 26. True to my impatient nature, I simultaneously experimented with a very streamlined hull and wings. Now it so happens that both these ideas, the streamlined hull with wings and the delta rig, have proven valid, but it probably was a mistake to link them in the same design. Sailors see what they think is a radical rig on what they think is a radical hull, and they have to make two leaps of faith—which is unlikely, because sailors are a conservative lot. With time they will come around, but only after they are quite convinced their friends won't think them foolish.

Let me assure you, without any real hope of immediately convincing you, that there is nothing radical about this rig—or even the Delta 26. The delta rig is merely a logical exploration of an overlooked possibility—the mast in the rear. Those looking for a dramatic breakthrough in performance are likely to be disappointed, because the delta rig is surprisingly normal in almost every respect. The big pluses are:

1. A mast arrangement that does not interfere with deck, cockpit, or cabin space.

2. A sail plan that can be entirely furled on efficient roller furlers, making it easily adjustable and supremely storable.

3. A rig that eliminates the danger of the boom bashing your head.

4. A rig that lets you get the same speed with less sail area, because all the sails have clean leading edges.

5. A rig that delivers some upward lift.

One of the things that makes the delta rig viable is the degree to which furling gear has improved. I happen to be partial to the excellent Harken product, but there are a number of good brands out there. It is very hard to beat the ease of furling as a solution for getting sail on and off quickly. Roller furling within or behind a mast is another story—none of the gear presently available really does a proper job in my estimation. The hide-away or stowaway mast destroys leading edge efficiency, and the flat, battenless sail that follows it is a sorry substitute for the power a proper sail can develop.

The Delta 26 shows a streamlined form adapted to its sailing function. Roller furling and the Spinnaker Gun Mount remove the need for going forward under sail, and the necessary deck space is achieved by wings adjoining the cockpit area.

Getting back to the Delta 26, its upwind performance is excellent and easy. Downwind, the genoa, like all genoas, very quickly twists off and becomes inefficient when eased out. Adding wings to get a wider sheeting base improves this situation, but the best complement is an easy spinnaker setup like the Hoyt Gun Mount. With the new roller-furling spinnaker for the Gun Mount, the delta rig offers furling convenience offwind as well as upwind. Pretty slick and very simple.

Staying the rig properly does pose a problem. You have to get backstay tension

54

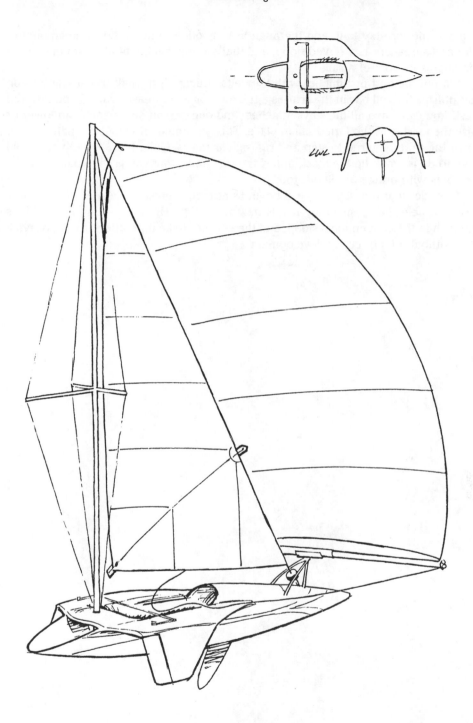

The MX, a fast singlehanded dinghy. In this design I'm using a roller-furling jib on a single wish-bone boom, and a roller-furling spinnaker on the Hoyt Gun Mount. Twin rudders are mounted off the wings.

to make the forestay taut, and the angle isn't good. You need the same amount of wire and spreaders as a stayed sloop, and that's a drawback, but at least none of the windage is in front of a sail.

One of the best possibilities with the delta concept is a small trailerable version that utilizes the roll bar in the rear as a fulcrum for a very easily raised and lowered mast. You can leave all the stays attached, and one person on a winch can lower or raise the mast with the furled sail in place. This arrangement would dramatically cut down the time required to step and rig regular masts. Quite literally, all you would have to do is crank up the mast, unfurl the sail, and away you go. It would be great for boats with bridge problems, too.

I predict that the delta rig will begin to attract interest because it offers a new way in a field that desperately needs new ways. The rig does a number of things better than the conventional sloop, and the gear to make it practical is readily available without a lot of costly development.

ELEVEN

The Freestanding Delta Sloop

As you have read, both the Freedom and delta rigs have their own quotients of vices and virtues. In line with my theory that there is always a better way, I decided to stop maligning the sloop, and instead see how it could be significantly improved. So here goes.

Two things are clear from looking around any harbor:

1. The sloop rig is preferred by a vast majority.
2. Furling gear is universally popular and practical.

Unquestionably the most popular rig today is the sloop. It has proven efficiencies and is very well accepted by racers and cruisers alike. The addition of new and better roller-furling gear has made the genoa a practical cruising sail, which has further enhanced the appeal of the sloop rig. It has, however, some significant drawbacks. At the risk of repeating a known litany:

1. The need for a highly tensioned forestay and backstay. The immediate by-products of this are enormous compression loads on the mast, plus large upward bending moments on the ends of the hull. This requires significant hull stiffening plus a variety of struts and wires to keep the highly compressed mast in column. The net is a highly tensioned (strained) rig with high windage from many wires.

2. Significant loss of aerodynamic efficiency resulting from mast interference on the mainsail, and the effect of a large clump of furled sail at the leading edge of

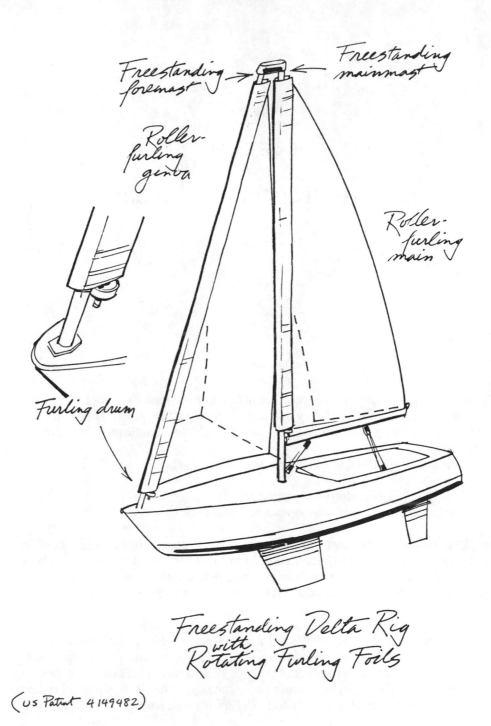

Freestanding foremast →

← Freestanding mainmast

Roller-furling genoa

Roller-furling main

Furling drum

Freestanding Delta Rig
with
Rotating Furling Foils

(US Patent 4149482)

The Freestanding Delta Sloop combines the ease of roller furling with the aerodynamic efficiency of a rotating wing mast.

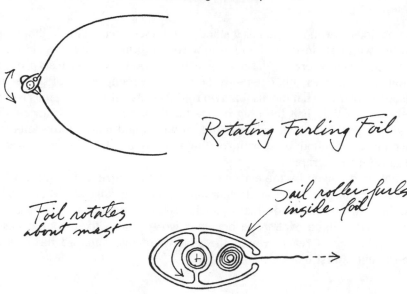

Rotating Furling Foil

Foil rotates about mast

Sail roller-furls inside foil

the jib. In its normal sailing condition (genoa jib plus main) the sloop rig suffers from a de-powered mainsail, since the mast and mast wires spoil the flow of clean air over the leading edge of the main. When the genoa jib is either partially or completely furled, its leading edge becomes a large, round, very nonaerodynamic element that is pure drag.

What I propose is a new approach to the sloop rig, one that builds on the aesthetic acceptance of the rig but corrects its present deficiencies. This new rig, which I dub the Freestanding Delta Sloop, is really two masts joined at the top. The mainmast is the vertical support element, which can be stepped through the deck in the normal fashion. The forward mast is stepped through or on the deck and is of sufficient diameter to take the backward load of the genoa and the forward load of the spinnaker. Thus, in effect, the Delta mast is a two-legged freestanding mast with the forward leg providing forward and rearward support. The result is a rig that is structurally stiff fore and aft, but free to bend to leeward.

The parallel that first springs to mind is again the airplane wing—very stiff in the fore and aft direction, but free to bend up and down, as can easily be observed from an airplane window. Anyone familiar with the freestanding mast has observed that it is not suitable for efficiently carrying a large jib, because the sidewards bend of the mast immediately induces sag in the forestay. This makes the jib fuller with an ever tighter leech, creating an undesirable shape as the wind increases. Yet it has been repeatedly demonstrated that the "swerve" effect—and the slot effect of the jib— make the sloop rig more effective to windward. *What the Freestanding Delta Sloop Rig does is to make the sloop feasible for the first time in freestanding form.* You get sidewards bend, but this only de-powers the sail slightly—a desirable result as the wind increases. The "forestay," being a foremast, does not sag, so the jib keeps its shape and its drive.

The obvious flaw in this plan as it stands is the increased windage that would be created by two masts instead of one, a flaw which, if uncorrected, could outweigh any benefits. This is where my Furling Foil comes in. Aerodynamic tests prove that a full airfoil shape creates only one-tenth the drag of a round shape of similar frontal width (see Chapter 3). That means that two round masts with rotating foils will create considerably less than half the drag of *one* fixed mast. Note that I am talking not about wing masts, but about foils rotating around round masts. Experiments have convinced me that round masts with rotating foils are a better way to go—easier to build and safer to operate.

Do not be deceived by the aerodynamic shape of current stayed masts. Being fixed on the centerline, these masts can only act aerodynamically when the boat is pointed directly into the wind—that is, anchored or in the middle of a tack. On any other course, the fixed oval shape becomes worse that a fixed round mast. It is particularly bad on a reach, where the shadow of mast-induced turbulence can trouble the entire first half of the sail.

The freestanding nature of both legs of the Delta Mast means they are uncluttered by wires or spreaders and can easily be equipped with the Rotating Airfoil Sleeve that also houses the furling gear. On the forward mast this foil would house the gear of a regular furling jib. In the case of the vertical mainmast, the rotating airfoil sleeve would house either a furling mainsail or a fully battened main operating on a track on the rear edge of the foil. It can be seen that this rig favorably harmonizes a lot of advantages.

Opposite page: The rotating airfoil sleeve can be used either with a roller-furling mainsail or in conjunction with the benefits of a fully battened main.

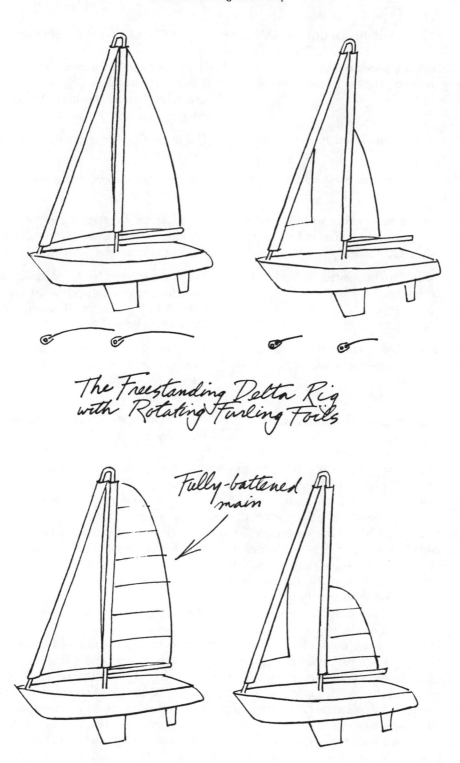

*The Freestanding Delta Rig
with Rotating Furling Foils*

Fully-battened
main

FREESTANDING DELTA SLOOP	REGULAR STAYED SLOOP
All surfaces presented to the wind are streamlined and working to create drive.	Many surfaces presented to the wind (mast and stays) which are neither streamlined nor working to create drive.
The overall profile shape is efficient.	The overall profile shape (triangular) is inefficient.
No excessive structural strain on the hull.	The rig imposes severe structural strain on the hull.
Jib can be self-tending with no loss in efficiency because mainsail foil insures leading edge efficiency.	Jib must be overlapping in order to attempt to restore airflow detached by mast interference.
All sails can be efficiently furled on rolled furlers.	Mainsail can only be furled via clumsy systems inside mast, prone to failure, difficult to fix, and highly inefficient at the leading edge.
More reliable because the number of potential failure points has been significantly reduced.	Less reliable because every wire, spreader, and end fitting represents a failure point that can demolish the whole rig.
Full-length battens are easily possible.	Full-length battens are prohibited by backstays.

This new Delta Sloop Mast system could be produced in four basic sizes with appropriately fitted rotating foil sections and furling gear. The Delta Mast might first be promoted to sailboat manufacturers as a critically needed means of providing new incentive for people to buy new boats. There is a secondary opportunity as a refit item for used boats, but care must be taken here to insure that there is proper strength at the deck partners. Partner strength is not always adequate on boats that were designed for supporting stays.

Properly produced, this rig is unquestionably simpler and more efficient than the present stayed sloop rigs. Properly promoted, it can become a desired rig because it does not violate accepted aesthetics while delivering demonstrable gains in convenience and efficiency.

The Delta Rig should be of special interest to multihulls, since catamarans in particular have a problem keeping headstay tension. Every time a hull moves the headstay loses tension, and trying to correct this involves complex and troublesome running backstays. It is intriguing to think that a "closed" Delta composed of three connected tubes could quickly solve that problem and also become a simple means of developing some extra upward lift to relieve downward pressure on the leeward hull. The wide staying base of the catamaran would enable a single set of adjustable side stays to angle the whole "closed Delta" to windward. The rig would maintain its fore-and-aft rigidity, insuring proper set of the sails, and the windward rake would further deliver the lift benefits already described.

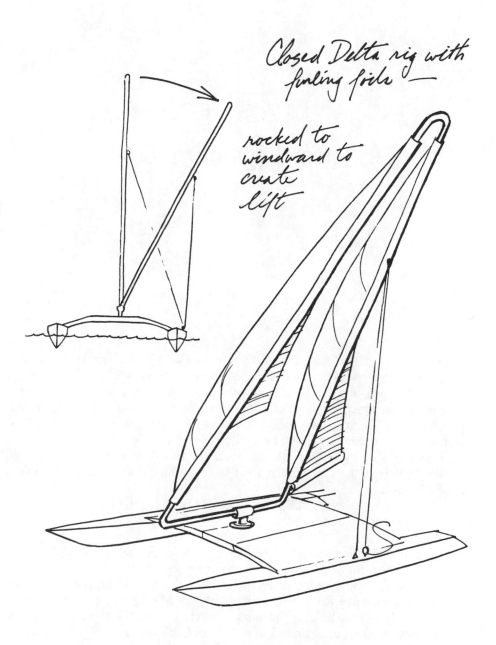

Closed Delta rig with furling foils —

rocked to windward to create lift

The simple expedient of inclining the rig to windward will directly improve the speed performance of multihulls, and assist in controlling dangerous heeling forces. The Closed Delta Rig makes a rigid shape that maintains foresail shape, and the furling foils make sail reduction easy and aerodynamic.

TWELVE

A Better Beginner's Boat

I earlier pointed out that sailing needs a new teaching instrument to ease more newcomers into the sport. I suggested that the proper criterion for this instrument is that it be a boat which a complete beginner could solo from a dock, around a triangular course, and back after just one hour of instruction. There is no question that the availability of such a boat would facilitate the development of new sailors, because it would vastly shortcut the long days of teaching that are now necessary to solo a beginner. And by making solo sailing easily attainable, this new boat would automatically correct the damaging impression that sailing is a dangerous, complex, and difficult sport.

While there is no shortage of small sailboats on the market, they just don't fit the bill for the following reasons:

1. Most of them tip over easily. Tipping over is OK for young kids who know how to swim. They can be persuaded that capsizing and righting a Sunfish is no big deal—and if you are young and know how to swim, it isn't. But you just are not going to get the average person, particularly the average woman, to try something that is going to tip over and dump her in the water. "Will it tip over?" is the first question nervous beginners ask. And *all* beginners are nervous. Since an honest answer to this query has to be affirmative for most small boats, these boats fail right at that point to attract beginners.

2. The boom is a potentially lethal instrument that can cause serious injury from an instant of neglect or error. If you are candid, you have to tell the beginner that

should he or she accidentally jibe, the boom will come across the deck with dangerous force. If he gets his head in the way (very easy to do), he's going to be hurt, possibly seriously. This makes a second strong turn-off, and the boom is standard equipment on virtually all sailboats. The ability to know when a jibe will occur, and then to prevent it, is not easy for a beginner to acquire. It requires knowing exactly where the wind is coming from and being able to keep the boat on a steady course—two entirely alien skills for the beginner. *If you have to warn them that they might get killed, they aren't going to try.*

3. Most small sailboats do not have adjustable sail area. Given the gamut of people's sizes and weights (from five feet and ninety pounds to six feet and two hundred and fifty pounds) plus the varying forces of the wind, there is no way one fixed sail area on a small boat can satisfactorily bracket the field of beginners. What is right for two hundred fifty pounds in fifteen knots of breeze is way too much for ninety pounds. And what's right for ninety pounds is way too little for two hundred and fifty pounds. Besides, the best way to teach anybody is to start with a little sail and let him personally add or subtract area as his confidence and ability grow.

It follows that our better beginners' boat has to begin by eliminating these primary negatives. It's not all that difficult—it just hasn't been done because nobody has thought through the problem in the necessary terms. I have, and my solution is the Solo.

1. The Solo is ballasted, which solves the tipping problem.

2. It has foam flotation, so it can't sink.

3. The rig is balanced, so the accidental jibe has been eliminated.

4. The boom is placed high up where it can't hit the head of a seated person, even if it happened to swing—which it won't because it's balanced.

5. The sail area is divided into a top sail and a low sail, both of which are completely adjustable in the manner of a window shade. You pull the top sail up and the low sail down.

6. Sail trim—the angle of the sail to the wind—is controlled by a tiller that rotates the mast. There are no sheets or lines to foul or confuse.

7. The plastic wind indicator on the bow is placed on a circular card, which is subdivided in colored or numbered segments.

8. A larger circular card with matching color segments is placed on the deck around the mast. This card is so designed that placing the mast tiller in the same color segment to which the wind direction arrow points will yield the correct sail trim.

9. In a computerized version, a computer would read the wind direction and automatically light up the appropriate segment, showing where the mast tiller should be placed.

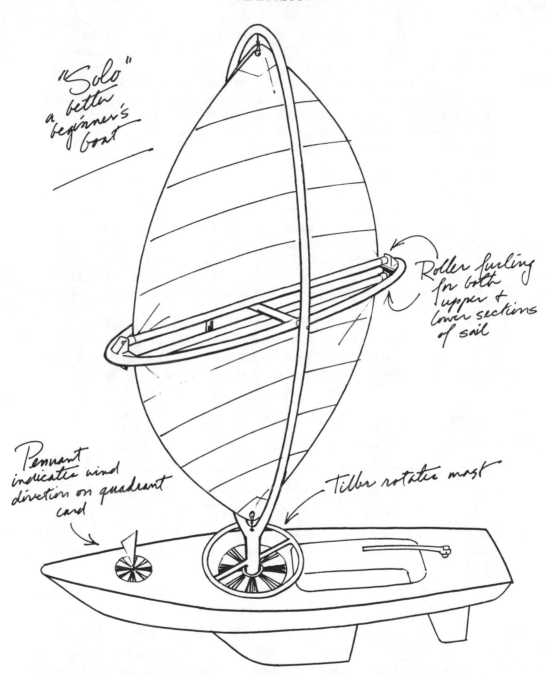

"Solo" a better beginner's boat

Roller furling for both upper + lower sections of sail

Pennant indicates wind direction on quadrant card

Tiller rotates mast

The Solo is designed to be a singlehander, but her 13-foot length can support two persons. The keel is ballasted so the boat can't tip, and foam in the bow and stern sections makes it unsinkable. You can't get hit with the boom, and if you just place the mast tiller over the color quadrant that matches the color quadrant the wind indicator points to, you get the correct sail trim angle. The top sail is pulled up—and the lower sail, down—in the manner of a windowshade. If you release either one of the halyards, the corresponding sail rolls itself up on its spring-loaded roller. With the help of an instructional video, I bet anyone can solo this boat in an hour.

It is my bet that with this boat plus a short, instructive videotape, any average person can solo in a reasonable breeze (under 20 miles per hour) in less than one hour. Sailing resorts equipped with the Solo would have the means for quickly turning people on to the pleasure of sailing. My frank hope is that some enterprising manufacturer and enterprising resorts will see this opportunity. It represents a needed catalyst for better growth.

At this point, a fair question might be, "Well, the Solo looks fine for getting a person to sail quickly and safely, but if they learn on that boat how are they going to handle all the other boats which will be their only choices in larger sizes?" A beginners' boat that is markedly simpler to operate is all well and good, but do we then just wish our graduating students lots of luck with all the more familiar, more complicated kinds of boats out there? I see this problem as a disguised opportunity. If there is one thing clear from today's sailing picture, it is that existing boat designs (over 20 feet) have not succeeded in attracting new people to the sport. So more of this same kind of boat is not the answer. Maybe—without denying the validity of existing designs— what we need is a whole new "branch" of sailing, a division that is significantly simpler in all size ranges.

The "Double Wishbone Rig" could be the key, because its balanced nature does away with all the ropes, lines, and winches that have obviously played a major role in turning most people off from sailing. With this rig on larger boats, it would clearly be possible to use a simple computer setup to link a given wind direction to the correct sail trim automatically. The rig, being balanced, can be turned easily at the mast base by a small amount of electrical power. The furling nature of the sails also enables them to be reefed or stowed quickly by electrical power. This means that all sail adjustments—hoisting, lowering, reefing, and trim—could be accomplished by one person from a control center at the wheel. A manual override, which could be a wheel within the wheel, would provide for manual trim control whenever needed or desired.

I realize this concept does violence to the sacraments of hauling, hoisting, trimming, winching, easing, and tweaking, but we must face the fact that most people see these operations as "work," and work is not what they go out on the water to do. Remember the axiom that relaxation is the first reason for, and benefit of, cruising. Work can indeed be relaxation, and most current sailors subscribe to the idea that the sailing motions of hiking and trimming are not "work" any more than hitting a tennis ball or skiing a slope can be termed "labor."

But not everybody sees it that way. I have taken a number of powerboat fans out sailing, and once you get squared away on a reach they really begin to enjoy it. They comment on the pleasure of silence and the nice "feel" of sailing along. But what they can't hack and won't hack is all the lines, wires, winches, and complications that sailors go through in order to get "squared away on a reach." If we are to have any hope of attracting this not-so-silent majority, we must devise ways to deliver sailing fun on *their* terms, not ours.

The basic pleasure in sailing is moving silently, in harmony with the wind. Any boat that does that is a sailboat, and anyone that sails that boat is a sailor. The reason there are roughly ten times as many powerboaters as sailors is that on powerboats one can turn the key, push the throttle, steer—and go. This preference does not

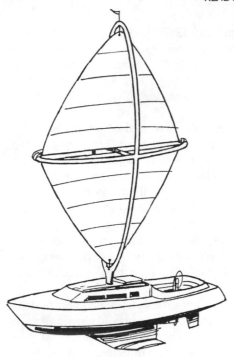

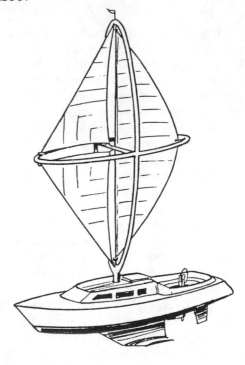

A 35-foot double-wishbone topsail cat.

A 35-foot double-wishbone topsail sloop.

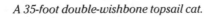

A 50-foot double-wishbone topsail schooner.

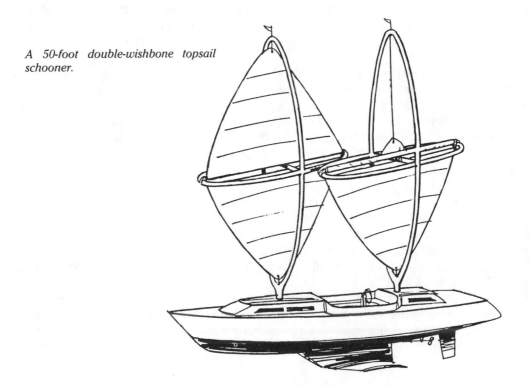

make powerboaters lazy slobs or power-mad stinkpotters—rather, it just means they are a group that likes to get out and around on the water as easily as possible.

Sailing will never be as fast or as easy as power, but sailing can come a lot closer than the limitations of present rigs allow. A whole new group of people, untouched by present sailing designs and practices, could be attracted by the prospect of a simple, successful solo in the right kind of beginners' boat. And they could be kept in the sport by a subsequent line of larger sailboats that did not lose sight of these same simplified features. Isn't it better to design a rig that lets people quickly "succeed" at sailing, than to insist on rigs that cause most people to fail—or worse, fail to try? I think a boat that is better to begin with can also be, for a lot of people, a better boat *to end up with*.

A new "branch" of simplified sailboats should not be viewed as a threat, designed in any way to condemn or replace existing sailboats. Rather, this new branch should be seen as fresh diversity, exactly what is needed to attract a new audience.

THIRTEEN

Sailing Resorts

*H*and in hand with the idea of a simplified kind of sailboat goes the idea of resorts that can deliver a sailing ambiance along with a sailing introduction and instruction. I really believe that this new kind of resort could represent an interesting financial opportunity for entrepreneurs, as well as a new source of sailors. And new sailors is the first thing that sailing needs.

Consider the facts. A number of reputable surveys confirm that amongst the general public, sailing is one of the "most desired sports." Over 60 percent of those interviewed have said that they would "like to know how to sail." Consider, too, the wide use of sailing shots in general advertising in order to lend glamour and appeal. Contrast this wide public acceptance with the miserably narrow reality—the less than one percent of the general populace that actually does sail—and you see a huge gap. Obviously, there is something missing, something that prevents a lot of people from indulging their stated desire to learn to sail or to become part of the sailing picture.

Ski resorts were the catalysts that enabled that sport to reach outside itself and take in newcomers. The ski resort formula was and is very simple:

1. A setting of natural beauty.
2. Graduated levels of participation (beginners' slope, intermediate, expert).
3. Rental equipment, so the initial experiment does not involve a lot of capital.
4. An attractive after-hours social life that is by itself sufficient to warrant experimentation.
5. Easy, nonintimidating, nonhumiliating instruction, with rapid solo gratification. (You learn to snowplow in about 15 minutes.)

70

6. A totally nonelitist approach, with no social barriers or exclusive restrictions.
7. An interesting array of specialized clothing, which dresses the user in a different way while simultaneously proclaiming his/her sporting prowess.
8. Equal appeal to men and women.

Via this formula, remote mountain ski locations have become self-contained, attractive destinations. They become considerably more than merely hotels, because they offer common access to a shared enthusiasm—an easy, natural means of social introductions that allows participants to meet and enjoy each other. Ski resorts offer the promise of healthy, pleasurable daytime activity, plus the prospect of interesting nighttime activity. They get the family business with the promise of the former, and the singles business with a combination of the former and the latter. They are spared the expense of nightclub entertainers, because the shared enthusiasm takes most of the guests' energies, and with what's left over they entertain themselves.

Sailing could do exactly the same thing. There are exceptionally attractive sailing sites available from Maine to Florida, in the Midwestern lakes, in the Western and Northwestern regions of the United States, and in other locations worldwide. It is not necessary to place a sailing resort in the midst of the most expensive real estate. The success of the Club Med has shown clearly that a relatively remote or isolated location can be part of the charm. The key is making available enough activities to keep people from getting bored. Nobody complains of boredom at the ski resorts as long as there is snow—and a wind supply is a lot more dependable than snow supply.

To be able truly to advertise that a weekend in an attractive resort would make you a solo sailor would yield a surprising number of new recruits, people whose interest is already there but has not been tapped because the existing means of introducing people to sailing are too complex and intimidating. New equipment, new teaching attitudes, and new, specialized sailing resort locations could change all that.

FOURTEEN

Getting Women into Sailing

*I*t used to be that cars were all bought by men, and women got to pick the colors. That has changed dramatically, and now women buyers represent almost 50 percent of the car market. Sailing, however, is still back in the Dark Ages in terms of interesting women as individual buyers. Yes, a number of women go sailing with their husbands, and yes, they frequently have veto power over a model they don't like. But no, women are not into sailing in significant numbers, nor do they represent a significant part of the individual buying market. This is the single biggest failure in the sailing world, and also the single biggest opportunity.

Look what female participation has done for golf, tennis, skiing, and horseback riding. Female recruits have roughly doubled the total participation in those sports from what it was years ago. Sailing, with its emphasis on touch and finesse, should be a natural for women. Indeed, the combination of female sensitivity at the helm and male beef on the lines should be the most effective formula for either racing or cruising. But of course that isn't the way it works. Is there a more common sight in sailing than the 200-pound gorilla hugging the wheel, shouting instructions to his 100-pound female companion about how to throw the 30-pound anchor? Heaven forbid that he should let go the wheel (probably the easiest job on board), because the wheel is somehow mixed up in the role of captain, which of course is his by divine right. There is not much in this scenario calculated to attract women.

The most sensible place to start is simply to ask women why they don't sail. My sample is small (25), but the responses quickly suggest a pattern. The answers were:

1. Expensive — 20
2. Difficult — 16

3. Dangerous — 12
4. A male sport — 10
5. Not interested — 5

Multiple responses produced more than 25 answers.

Obviously, a more in-depth questionnaire would be appropriate, and might reveal other underlying causes. But right there on the surface are four devastating negatives, any one of which could knock the sport out of consideration. These four negatives should come as no surprise, because we persistently promote sailing as expensive, difficult, dangerous, and for males only. A review of the yearly calendar recently put out by one of the leading magazines showed thirteen scenes, twelve of which were all-male and eight of which gave a dominant impression of danger, complexity, and difficulty. The argument raised in defense of this policy is that such scenes make the most arresting visuals in the same sense that ski magazine covers often show dramatic slalom turns or speed runs and jumps. There is of course a point here, and to get the interest of the current market, which is predominantly male, it is probably quite effective to show just what the magazines do show—basically action shots of men on boats.

The problem is that this approach does absolutely nothing to address the number one problem/opportunity, the need to attract women to sailing. The solution is not tame shots showing females on tranquil boats in quiet harbors—that's just dull, and would lose male interest without gaining female interest. A better approach would be to adopt the same policy that general advertising uses for minorities. You literally cannot find a group shot involving any product that doesn't religiously show a black, Oriental, or Hispanic. Granted, this often seems a bit forced, but the theory is very sound: How are blacks, Orientals, and Hispanics going to be accepted as bankers, surgeons, or fashion models unless they are depicted in those roles? And since advertising is a controlled, staged ambiance, why not at least stage things the way they ought to be?

Of course the answer to our question is not as simple as just changing the cover shots on sailing calendars and magazines. That's just a start, and you need a whole program. But it is at least a start, and since this kind of campaign takes time in any case, why not at least start with the parts you can stage? Programs of simpler sailing instruction with quicker solo rewards, plus promotion of weekend sailing resorts where a sailing experiment can be easily and economically indulged—all these things could be aimed directly at new female participation. There are proven ways of finding out exactly what females (or any group of people, for that matter) want; given that knowledge, the solution becomes a process of making sure the desired features are included both in the products and in new programs.

The best answers any man can offer will probably start off being second-best to what any number of smart women could provide, and getting smart women to work on this project is undoubtedly the best way to start.

FIFTEEN

Is Sailing a Sport or a Recreation?

Well, it's both. High-pressure class racing is certainly a sport, and has Olympic recognition as such. Leisurely daysailing, on the other hand, is a recreation whose practitioners probably consider it a sport, and that would also apply to the cruisers. If the problem were merely one of semantics, all this would be little ado about nothing. But the organizations that have to do with the "sport" of sailboat racing have exercised a disproportionate role that has managed to confuse and impede the attraction of sailing as a recreation. Were the "sport" of sailboat racing in a state of explosive or even steady growth, the dominant role of those organizations might be excused or justified. But it isn't, and they are in fact presiding over the marked decline of the very branch of sailing that is most dear to their hearts. To top off the disarray, the "yacht racing" establishment is currently engaged in an awkward, clandestine affair with the commercial world. They can't seem to bring themselves to openly ask the girl to dance, let alone couple in the closer fashion one suspects they both need and wish.

This unbecoming hesitancy has given rise to an unfortunate situation in which professional racing sailors pretending to be amateurs impinge on the recreational pleasure of the real amateurs who make up the majority of the sport. The result is sharply defined in the marked decline of class-racing participation—a sector of the sport that has always relied for its numbers primarily on weekend club racers.

The institutions in which sailors have traditionally placed their trust seem curiously blind to this plight of the average sailor who is the core of the sport. The yachting establishment wastes a great deal of time and energy piously blocking the overt appearance of commercialism, and then contradicting that by continuously allowing participants whose drive and methods are purely professional. Sailing thus finds itself in the plight of the Gooney Bird of World War II fame, which flew in ever smaller circles until it finally disappeared up its own obsessions.

"What," you might ask, "has all or any of this got to do with the daysailors or cruisers who make up the majority?" Well, class racing has always had an importance to sailing that far exceeded its actual numbers. Class racing was the best developer of better sailing skills, and it provided a steady seeding ground for sailors who later went on to all levels of daysailing and cruising. So this is not the time to ask for whom the bell tolls. To make the sport/recreation of sailboat racing more pleasurable to amateur participation, we must expurgate the professional element. The best way to do this is not to curse them or pretend they are not there, but rather to create a separate arena where they can have at each other on equal professional terms, for interesting professional rewards, with exciting spectator benefits.

The way to begin all this is by openly coming to grips with commercialism, even though one is hard put to like the sound of it. We already face too many commercials on television, unsightly billboards unnecessarily scar our countrysides, and tasteless advertising seems to assault the senses at every turn. Do we really want or need to invite this element into the sport/recreation that we often undertake expressly to remove ourselves from these landlocked irritations?

Well, no, I don't think anybody wants advertising or commercial presence for its own sake. But I suspect many would like the benefits that can accrue from an intelligent utilization of commercial involvement. First, let's isolate what we are talking about—and what we are not talking about.

We are talking about inviting commercial sponsors to pay for selected sailing competitions and events, and to make it worth their while we will have to be prepared to accept changes in the way yachting events are traditionally run, the equipment in which they are sailed, and the classification of those who enter. These are not cosmic changes; rather, in most cases, they are simply realistic adjustments that have already been made by sports such as golf, tennis, skiing, and fishing. Commercialism also offers a practical means of solving the aforestated problem of removing professionals from the amateur ranks, because it gives them a place to go.

It will almost always be true that whatever changes commercial sponsors require will be changes that also make the sport more interesting to the public—because public response is what commercial sponsors are interested in. And increased public response plus more promotional money is what the sport needs to:

1. Create more public interest and thereby create more new sailors.
2. Create the separate professional arena that the preservation of the existing amateur sport requires.
3. Stimulate new design innovation.

Those who prefer to view sailing/yachting as the privileged province of a chosen few will almost certainly be offended by commercial sponsors, whose first intent is to make popular what the exclusives view as private. On the other hand, opening up the commercial end of sailing will certainly leave room for those clubs and organizations who choose to remain as private and traditional as they have always been. In fact, having commercial/professional channels open and accepted will free private clubs from the present awkward straddle whereby obvious professional participation has to be winked at, and frequent covert commercial support is thinly disguised as Corinthian.

As I see it, the present pretense that sailing is only an amateur sport puts heavy pressure on the truth, without any specific gains and some rather specific losses and dangers, as have been previously described. Open and legitimate commercial sponsorship of selected events and open recognition and separation of professional talent will immediately accelerate design development with resulting spinoff benefits to all members of the sailing public. Shedding the sham of an amateur purity whose benefits are no longer clear nor practical could be like shedding the lead that so burdens current design thought. The very action opens up new possibilities, and I believe sailing needs that fresh air. I also believe that sailing has less to fear from commercial involvement than from its present policies of elitist neglect.

I can admit there is a part of me that says sailing should be like poetry—there for its own beauty and not sullied by crass commercial concerns. But then I remind myself that Shakespeare was a commercial writer whose first worry was to fill the theater next week, and Michelangelo was a commercial painter working for the pope, who often dictated both his subject matter and technique. Working to please more of the general public is what commercialism forces, and that is a pretty good description of what sailing needs right now. We have already seen what an unrecognized and therefore uncontrolled professionalism can do to poison the ranks, and commercialism is creeping in one way or another. Better to harness both professionalism and commercialism in ways that can clearly benefit the sport by forcing new design development and forging new public interest, than to sit back and let things slide. The sport/recreation of sailing is not "above" commercialism—it needs commercialism to do things that sailing has been conspicuously unable to do for itself.

SIXTEEN

The Curse of the Olympic Course

At the Beachwood Yacht Club on Tom's River, New Jersey, where I grew up and learned to sail, there was only one starting line. It was a buoy permanently located about 50 yards off the yacht club dock, and it was also the finish line. This arrangement was based firmly on several practical facts:

1. Most of the boats were either located or launched right at the club, so they had to start out there and finish there.

2. Having the race committee stand on the dock made them easily accessible to all the sailors and eliminated the expense and nuisance of a committee boat.

3. Spectators could easily view and enjoy the two most exciting moments of racing—the start and the finish.

4. Between-race operations such as lunch, boat repairs, sail changes, or trips to the head were all easy, because the shore facilities were right there.

Somewhere along the line, the common sense of all this was shattered by the notion, puritanically pursued, that all proper starts must be to windward. With papal certainty it was proclaimed that the starting line must be square to the wind to insure an even contest. A high percentage of windward work was de rigueur, and proximity to shore was declared to be evil—rife with shifty winds and other subversive forces. The Olympic course was prescribed as the only true way, and since the space necessary for that sacred geometry was never available near the yacht club, the whole race operation moved offshore.

The first result of this policy was a direct rise in the cost and complexity of race operations, accompanied by an equally direct decline in spectator interest. Who can enjoy a race when you can't see the start and the finish? Race committees suddenly sprouted blue blazers, white caps, and gold braid. Enthroned on expensive yachts, they have become imperiously aloof and impervious to ordinary sailor questions such as, "How much time to the start?" or, "What's the course?" Vocal communication in plain English became illegal if not extinct—all is flags, clocks, cannons, and a shroud of secrecy disguised as propriety. Great store is set on getting the line right, and attempting this rarely achieved feat is generally good for the wasting of at least thirty minutes. Add to this the half hour it now takes to get out to the starting line, and you have a new hour of nonracing. Shoreside spectators can only see white dots bobbing on the horizon, so they have stopped watching what they can't enjoy.

Maybe it's time we rethought what we have gained versus what we have lost by this obsession with windward starts and Olympic courses. Few would argue the desirability of the Olympic course for national or international championships. Where visitors are involved, the race course has to be made as familiar and as neutral as possible. Taking the races to open waters reduces the need for local knowledge and evens the scales for all the sailors.

But for local races, what is really wrong with the yacht club start and finish? It takes every bit as much and maybe even more skill to get a good downwind or reaching start. By reducing the time needed for setup you get more time for racing. Spectators are invited back into the picture, and what better way to attract new participants than to show them a congenial, easily accessible sport instead of a distant clutter of sails on the horizon. In addition, let's bring the actual racing course back closer to land, by setting buoys in coves and close to points, so people who are interested can see what's going on during the race.

One of the best ways to attract new interest to the sport of sailboat racing is to give it better visibility. This is not accomplished by sailing over the horizon in the pursuit of artificial race course purity. If the sport could be relieved of some of the difficulties we have legislated onto it, it would immediately emerge as a more likable pursuit.

The extent and complexity of the racing rules is another offshoot of the over-seriousness we have insisted on attaching to sailing events. Rules by themselves have no importance; they only exist to the degree to which they can help insure or improve the enjoyment of the sport. Alas, sailing rules and rule-making seem to have taken on a life of their own, and the mere beginner is justifiably made hesitant by the sheer volume of technicalities he is supposed to understand and obey. Since rules and restrictions have absolutely no value in terms of attracting people to the sport, we should endeavor to develop a minimum set for beginner or amateur racing. For example, supposing we divided the fleet in two and equipped half the fleet with big red flags. We might then operate by two simple rules:

1. Starboard tack always has right of way.
2. In close situations, boats with red flags have the right of way. For the next race, boats without red flags would have the right of way, and thus advantage would be canceled out.

"That's it. That's all you have to know. Let's go!"

I realize this sounds far too simple, but what has happened is that race course bureaucrats have begun to have the same effect on sailboat racing that bureaucrats have on anything. The sport has become unduly complicated—more pompous and less pleasurable because of the weight of well-intentioned rules and restrictions. We complain about a litigious society, but our race course arena has been pointlessly confused by an ever expanding mass of incomprehensible technicalities. We now have rules experts who pride themselves on their ability to disqualify those of lesser knowledge, and they often win races thereby.

Of course, they can only win via the protesting process, which is another weight and delay we have imposed on the pleasure and comprehensibility of racing.

Think for a minute. Tennis and golf at the amateur level are almost completely controlled by the assumed honesty of your opponents. Sure, some tennis players call balls out that are really in, and some golfers cheat to improve their lie, but by and large the system works. In sailboat racing we have insisted on providing a rule to cover every crossing and meeting situation between boats on the water. The result is an intricate maze of fluid rights that are subject to judgmental discretion during the race and whose disposition must be decided by involved committee decisions after the race.

Elementary courtesy and basic sportsmanship are the first victims vanquished by our racing rules. We have reached the point at which, if you view even a harmless, nonmalicious, minor collision that has no effect on the race, you must report it or risk disqualification yourself. This fosters a KGB mentality and elevates the manipulation of rules to an importance far beyond what they deserve.

The extent and complexity of our racing rules cause them to intrude upon what they are supposed to protect—the pleasure of sailing. Furthermore, the protest process delays and obscures race results to the direct detriment of spectator interest.

Let's reassess. We don't need a system that provides a rule to cover every situation. We need a system that *doesn't require a rule to cover every situation.* And the sooner the better.

Studying a rule book may be fun for some people, and writing them must obviously be fun for other people. But if we want to get the public more into the sport we should, in sailor's language, take about 60 percent of the rules and shit-can them.

SEVENTEEN

The Risks of Misguided Technology

*T*he USA is a nation that worships technology, and improved technology is often seen automatically as the means to a better end. Technology certainly does make better things possible, and in the world of sports we have seen dramatic improvements in equipment that definitely raised both the safety levels and the enjoyment of the sport. Look how the new skis and the new ski boots have virtually transformed that sport, making it more glamorous and considerably easier and safer than it once was.

But in ocean and one-design sailboat racing we have now come to the point at which the new primary skill seems to be the ability to select, install, and adjust increasingly complex equipment. No one can question that this is a skill, and that some have it more than others. What we should question is whether this is a sensible course for a sport, if growth in public participation forms any part of the program.

It is hard to think of any sport other than car racing in which the selection and adjustment of equipment is the primary factor in competitive success. Car racing can support this complication, because car racing is commercially aimed at high public interest but low public participation. The high public interest comes as a result of the unremitting focus on speed, plus careful staging to make car racing events constantly viewable and enjoyable to the spectator. For these reasons, car racing is interesting to commercial sponsors, who put up the money that keeps the whole thing running. High public interest attracts sponsors, who then work hard to stage events and keep public interest up because that's the only way to justify their investment.

A large part of competitive sailing has fallen into the trap of high technical complexity without either the lure of substantial speed or the promise of viewer enjoyability. This is a dangerous no-man's-land because it guarantees you will get neither significant public participation nor significant commercial support.

There is a simple law that operates here. When the importance of the equipment begins to outweigh the skill of the operator, the number of participants will directly decrease. This is because success shifts from a dedication of individual time and effort (a matter of personal commitment) to an application of dollars (a matter of financial resources). My view is that when the importance of the equipment outweighs the skill of the operator, a sport ceases to be a sport and becomes a technology.

There are important distinctions to be drawn here. No one would suggest that an Olympic javelin champion wins because he has a better javelin. Carl Lewis did not run to four gold medals on the basis of better shoes. Nor do the kayaks or shell champions win because of any compelling difference in their equipment. Guns and bows and racquets and golf clubs have improved, but the dollar factor has not gotten out of hand, so superior equipment is standard and operator skill remains the determining factor in winning. Equestrian? Well, there's no denying you have to have a good horse to win. I've always felt that the medals should be given to the horses, but there at least we are dealing with natural power, which is somehow pleasingly different from "equipment power."

I have watched Buddy Melges, arguably the best sailor in the world, relatively helpless at the helm of a technically inferior IOR boat. I have seen Dennis Connor clearly outsail the Australian contingent in the 1983 America's Cup, with better starts and better tactics, but still lose because his equipment was inferior. If this phenomenon were limited to the upper stratosphere of IOR or twelve-meter racing, it might be dismissed as merely part of those esoteric games. But the tendency has crept downward into the one-design classes as well. Today, professional technicians, mostly sailmakers, can move from class to class and dominate because of their better ability to purchase and adjust the best equipment. Of course these technicians also tend to be excellent sailors, but mere sailing skill will no longer suffice to win. I think that's too bad, because a sport is a lot more fun than a technology. And a lot more people will sign up for a sport than will ever sign up for a technology.

One of the great pleasures of Sunfish racing is that the technology of the object is so primitive, and the adjustable options so limited, that you are forced to rely almost entirely on sailing skills. The Laser is similarly restrained in its adjustment scope, and this is a large part of the reason why so many excellent sailors come from these classes. Also, and significantly, there is more sailing time and fun because the distraction of equipment adjustment has been removed.

Boardsailing has developed so rapidly that there is indeed a premium on the latest technology. But as a factor in race success, the skill of the operator still far outweighs the nuances between one top brand and another. Perhaps more than with any other sail craft, the athletic skill of the boardsailor is dramatically and pleasingly evident.

The problem of technology taking the bit is intertwined with sailing's hypocrisy in treating the fact of today's "semipros" or "pseudo-amateurs." If we had a genuine, recognized professional circuit, it would very quickly adapt itself to the needs of a spectator sport—meaning an uncluttered quest for speed, and sensible accommodations to create a viewable sport. The need to make money, or the desire to make more, would soon dispense with a lot of the folderol. As car racing has shown, there is no particular problem with technology dominating a professional sport, because it is designed to have a few highly trained practitioners entertaining a large number of nonparticipating spectators.

But when you want more participants you must keep the equipment subordinate to the operator, both to keep the cost in line and to keep reasonable competence within the grasp of the amateur, who has only his after-work hours to apply to the pursuit.

The best way to move the pros out of amateur sailing is to create a more lucrative area for them to practice their more sophisticated skills. There is no trouble keeping Chris Evert Lloyd out of the amateur ranks, because she has far better fish to fry in the pro ranks. Closer to home, the boardsailors have created their own professional ranks, and the likes of Robby Naish don't bother the amateur sailboarders at all.

Think how easily the words "golf pro," "tennis pro," and "ski instructor" roll off our lips. In most cases these descriptions do not apply just to superstar professional performers; rather, they often refer to a large corps of skilled professional practitioners who simply teach other people the sport. This is a missing element in sailing. The closest we come is the summer sailing instructor at the yacht club, and that is too elite and too restricted a funnel to create interesting growth. There have recently been some new moves afoot to create national professional standards for sailing instructors, and this is all to the good. We need sailing pros to make sailing skills more easily acquirable.

Still missing from the equation is a better piece of teaching equipment, as per my earlier chapter on the subject. Also missing is the equivalent of either the public tennis court (or golf course) or the ski resort—an area where interested recruits can quickly and easily be surrounded by the ambiance of the sport, and enjoy the after-hours social activity that can be as much of an incentive as actual participation in the sport.

Rather than directing technology to improve the accessibility, safety, and enjoyment of the sport, sailing has allowed technology to become a complicating factor that hugely increases the sport's cost and complexity and consequently lowers its attractiveness to the general public. The overemphasis on the selection and adjustment of equipment has also tended to reduce the value of pure sailing skills, which, though still vital, can no longer be considered the primary element of success on today's race courses. This, I submit, is a misguided use of technology. The modern sailboat racer is coming to rely more on banks of instruments and an array of adjustable equipment, and less on how to steer the boat and trim the sails by his own trained instincts. This amounts to a distortion of the skills that founded the sport: the ability to better sense the wind and steer and trim to the fastest course.

When the ability to purchase and adjust expensive equipment dominates, simple skills degenerate and interest declines. A sport that ignores this does so at its own risk.

EIGHTEEN

A New One Design Racing Class

The decline in one-design sailboat racing in the U.S. is lamented by all who recall this as perhaps the purest form of sailing pleasure, and an unmatched means for sharpening skills. As has been mentioned, the intrusion of professionalism and the privileged access to better equipment seem to have eroded the basic equality that was the primary strength and appeal of one-design sailing, and this problem needs to be addressed. But to see any sort of dramatic turnaround, we need to come up with some exciting design alternatives—both to attract newcomers and to lure back those who have left the ranks.

The numbers prove that the best organizing job in terms of one-design popularity has been done by manufacturers—Sunfish, Lasers, and Hobie Cats being leading examples. This ought to tell us something, mainly that the public interest (which is best measured by the popularity of a design) is most effectively served when those in charge of class rules and events have commercial interests and disciplines at stake. To build a class by bringing in a lot of builders—each of whom seeks a loophole in a set of rules drawn up by amateur committees with no grasp of manufacturing realities—is clearly not the way to go. Nor is baptizing a class with the artificial enhancement of Olympic status any guarantee of success, as the ill-fated Tempest quickly demonstrated. There are pockets of success in the present scene, of course, and classes like the Star, Snipe, Lightning, Thistle, J-24, and E-Scow continue to offer excellent regattas, but the overall number of participants is depressingly down. Since there are plenty of one-design classes out there already, the evidence is that we don't need just one more to add to the clutter. Rather, what we require is a design that does something the present classes can't or won't do.

To set the stage, we should identify where the most prominent designs have succeeded, and where they have lost their way. Let's begin with sustained applause for all of those classic classes that have endured and will endure. While thus paying proper respect, however, we must grant that the combined and varied virtues of all of them have not been sufficient to arrest the overall decline in one-design racing. So where and how have these excellent designs failed?

I believe a large part of the answer lies in extreme weight, sex, and age sensitivity. Particularly in the case of smaller craft like the Sunfish (220,000 sold) and the Laser (120,000 sold), operator weight is critical to performance. Usually there is no way a 200-pound skipper can make a Laser win in light winds, and conversely, there is no way a 120-pound skipper can win in heavy winds. This drawback is a tough one to solve, because the operator's weight is the righting arm that stabilizes these boats. In heavy winds you need a big righting arm, but in light winds a smaller righting arm is sufficient and better. A weight of 160 pounds comes closest to the ideal for handling both light and heavy winds, and this is tough on people who don't happen to weigh just that. To this factor we must add the age and sex sensitivity of these classes. Neither older nor female sailors can effectively compete against younger males whose better agility and upper body strength give them a specific advantage in the critical areas of hiking and kinetics. This narrow winning profile (young, male, 160 pounds) causes all others to lose races consistently, regardless of sailing skill—and this leads to a rapid loss of interest. Separate divisions could be an answer, but the sailing population is too small to afford the complications that would involve.

It would be a simple solution if those sailors outside the narrow physical ideal could just move on to some other class, but it doesn't work that way. A large percentage of them are not forever upwardly mobile—either in the scope of their interest or the scope of their income. What they would really go for is a simple but exciting singlehanded boat in which they could remain reasonably competitive at nearly any age. That is not presently possible, and because of this these sailors often drop out and take up another activity. They are not likely to settle for just crewing on a larger boat. Anybody who has been his own skipper finds it difficult to enjoy perching on a wet rail, staring blankly at the horizon, while another skipper of lesser skills drives the boat slowly to the wrong side of the course. It's just not the same kind of fun—if indeed it can be called fun at all.

So singlehanding remains a permanent attraction, and this creates a tempting target: to make a large one-design class—accessible to any sailor—which could shore up this type of racing at the most basic level without interfering with the fine classes already out there. And maybe, if done right, this new class could serve as a bridge between the presently diverging boardsailors and those who prefer more conventional sailing boats. Let's talk for a minute about sailboards, because to have any chance at all, our new class has got to include some of their newly discovered speed and excitement.

To acquire proper respect for the genius of Hoyle Schweitzer and Jim Drake's Windsurfer concept, one has only to sit down and try to think of something better. I admit that several years of intense mental drilling in that direction have brought me up remarkably dry, so I have to begin by registering my respect for their ingenuity. When you consider the formidable array of assets combined in the sailboard, it makes a compelling package:

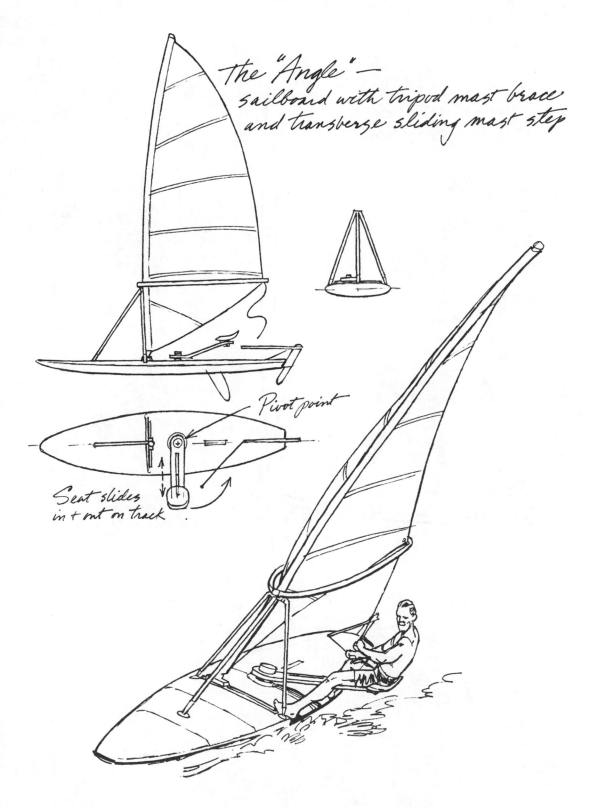

The "Angle" —
sailboard with tripod mast brace
and transverse sliding mast step

Pivot point

Seat slides
in + out on track

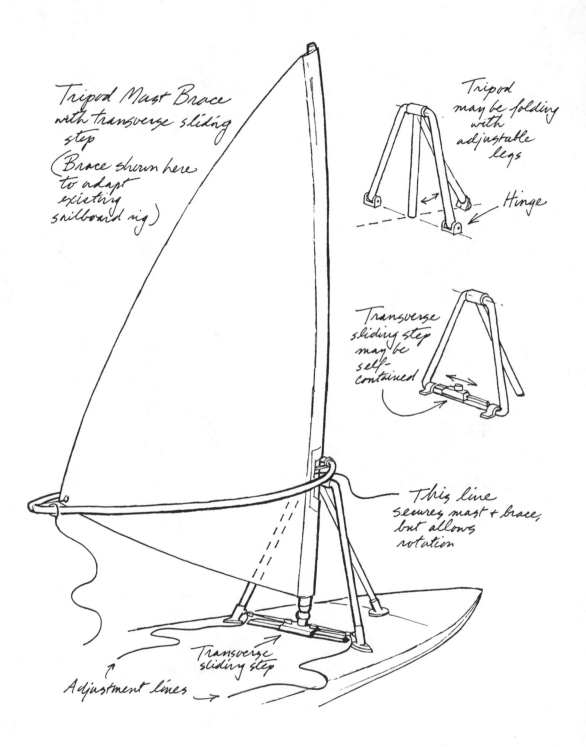

Tripod Mast Brace
with transverse sliding
step
(Brace shown here
to adapt
existing
sailboard rig)

Tripod
may be folding
with
adjustable
legs

Hinge

Transverse
sliding step
may be
self-
contained

This line
secures mast + brace,
but allows
rotation

Transverse
sliding step

Adjustment lines

1. Affordability
2. Portability (specifically, cartop-ability)
3. The conversion of heeling moment to upward lift by angling the sail to wind-ward. (I suspect this virtue was more serendipitous than planned—but there it is.)
4. Dramatic speeds that can reach over 30 mph.
5. Dropping the rig immediately stops the boat and keeps it from drifting.
6. Automatic camaraderie with an open club that can operate off any beach.
7. Solid non-leaking hulls that require little or no maintenance.
8. The most technologically advanced rigs and sails in the sailing world, with worldwide pressure steadily applied to improvement.

Paradoxically, this unquestioned excellence of innovation has not translated to significant one-design success. In many ways this is the inevitable result of the type's rapid technological progress. This factor has produced a bewildering abundance of sailboards—each with specific attributes, but no one of them able to deliver the even competition of a strong one-design class. You can't fault progress, but conversely you cannot build a strong one-design class on the basis of constant change.

Another complicating flaw in the brilliance of the Windsurfer concept is the difficulty of learning. No matter how you slice it, boardsailing is not something anybody does on the first try. Acquiring the necessary skill is perhaps most difficult of all for the adult male with previous sailing experience. He comes burdened with a high center of gravity, is probably overweight, and, worst of all, carries a surplus of pride in his knowledge and ability to sail. These factors combine to make his first sally on a sailboard a predictable public comedy wherein the once-proud hero is promptly unveiled as a clumsy buffoon. Small children and totally inexperienced women will quickly pass him by because they start out with less weight, a lower center of gravity, and a willingness to do precisely what they are told. Such is the delicacy of the male ego that after their first and usually thorough humiliation, most men will give up in disgust what they cannot quickly master. It is a commercial reality that you don't make a customer by starting him off as a laughing stock, and finding a way to better link sailboard performance to conventional sailing skills would be a big help—a missing link, if you will.

Then too, boardsailing may have gone a bit astray in the pursuit of exotic extremes. There is no question that leaping tall waves in a single bound makes great videos, and this end of the sport will always attract highly skilled daredevils whose maneuvers equally defy gravity and common sense. But it does not do to confuse these exploits with the interests of the common man or woman, who has neither the skill nor the inclination for such extremes. What seems to have been left behind or forgotten is the possibility that a standard one-design board could carry a young sailor through his or her growth period—from 80 pounds to 180 pounds—just by adding progressively larger new rigs. Such a one-design board would not pretend to beat the exotic boards at their specialties, but it would definitely come out the winner in terms of all-around value and durability.

A further, and simple, way to reduce sensitivity to operator weight is to increase the length of the hull or board. Although this opposes the trend to smaller sailboards that have proven faster and better for wave-jumping, length has compensating advantages, not the least of which is the way it quickly smooths out differences in operator weight. Modern materials make an increase in length possible without a heavy weight penalty, so portability would not be substantially altered in a longer board.

But the real key to one-design sailing equality is for all participants to use a standard, longer board and to *combine* this with specific sail area limits matched to the operator's weight. This would provide compensating fairness because the bigger loads are given more horsepower, and the lesser loads are given less horsepower. With this system, lightweights can be competitive in heavy winds, and heavyweights can be competitive in light winds. This feature of elementary fairness has heretofore not been available in any small one-design class, and it deserves a try. Mandatory sail area limits could be defined in terms of 20-pound increments in operator weight, with each sail plainly marked by the manufacturer.

My feeling is that hull development in sailboards, after years of explosive growth, has stabilized: the forms which produce good performance are now well known, and future stylistic variations will be designed more to move new boards at the sales level than to make significant improvements in performance.

In view of this, I decided to create a new design that would use the better wind engines (rigs) developed by sailboards in ways that not only would be less taxing to the beginner, but would not penalize weight, age, and sex differences so heavily. The most difficult part of learning to boardsail is acquiring the ability to harmonize the heeling and steering forces so that you can simultaneously stay upright and go where you want to go. So, let's devise a board boat that keeps you from repeatedly falling down, allows you to steer in the ordinary way with a rudder and tiller, and still delivers sailboard affordability, portability, lift, speed, camaraderie, and utilization of efficient rig.

My solution is a design called the "Angle"—so named because it enables you to angle the rig to windward in order to convert heeling moment to lift. But rather than employ the free-sail system, which requires the patented universal joint at the mast step, this solution provides for a folding tripod mast brace on the deck, with a transversely sliding mast step. You sit on a pivoting, sliding seat that maximizes your weight as balance, while also keeping your tail out of the water, and minimizes the need for hiking strength. You steer with a rudder and tiller in the normal manner from a comfortable seated position, and the rig is adjusted to windward by lines that run through the seat pivot post and are thus within easy reach. The tripod mast brace folds flat when not in use, while in the upright position it supports any sailboard rig by means of a line passed around the mast at the sail opening provided for the wishbone boom attachment. The butt of the mast sits in a cup on the transverse traveler, which provides the windward adjustment. The Angle, at 16 feet, is substantially longer than most sailboards. But new materials make it possible for a board to be very light, strong and durable, and this longer board would still be much lighter than a Laser or a Sunfish and could easily be carried on a cartop and transported by hand to the water. The Angle should definitely be faster than either the Sunfish or the Laser, and the sliding seat will widen the spectrum of participants to include those whose best hiking days are behind them, as well as those who are lighter or slighter in physique.

But the tantalizing benefit is that through combining the unique virtues of sail-boards with conventional steering and a sliding seat, and adding the new concept of matching sail area to operator weight on a standard board, we could create a basic one-design racing class whose performance capabilities would be exciting enough to keep the young people involved while not so physically exacting as to drive older or female participants out. For local one-design fleets, this might circumvent the present problem of young students starting out in some small boat only to drop out later for lack of a more exciting but still inexpensive boat to progress to. This safe, nonintimi-dating boat would have the performance potential to excite people of all descriptions. It would be, you might say, a better Angle. Hey, with this boat I might get back on the race course!

NINETEEN

Design Rules, Ratings and Restrictions

***I*OR (International Offshore Rule)**

There is nothing inherently wrong in the idea of competition limited to a small group composed of wealthy owners who buy expensive yachts, which are rendered obsolete every year and are crewed by professionals pretending to be amateurs. This arrangement provides financial nourishment to a number of naval architects, sailmakers, and custom boatbuilders, as well as considerable ego nourishment to the owners, who can enjoy the exclusivity of a competition whose yearly expenses often run to several hundred thousand dollars per boat. Arranging to have the primary American race circuit (SORC) in Florida during the winter months is a nice touch that guarantees excessively extensive coverage by the American yachting press, which, being centered in the Northeastern United States, is desperately grateful for any excuse to depart from the uncivilized conditions of a New England winter. The only problem comes in the resulting pretense that this IOR racing has anything much to do with superior sailing skill or meaningful design progress. By giving IOR racing center-stage importance, we are merely publicizing an image that reinforces the negative perceptions that are hobbling the sport, without in any way making the kind of significant speed progress that could begin to expand the sport's horizons. In short, there is nothing wrong with the IOR except the media focus put upon it.

MHS (Measurement Handicap System)

This is an exhaustively conceived formula for mathematically assessing the performance potential of sailboats. The problem is that it takes a lot of time and money, and the results to date have been disappointing in terms of perceived fairness. I would rate MHS as an excellent effort, but one yearns for a simpler solution.

PHRF (Performance Handicap Racing Fleet)

When I first heard about PHRF, I thought we had arrived at the promised land. After all, here was a rating system that did not attempt to dictate or influence design— rather, it would simply handicap objectively on the basis of performance. Alas, it was not that simple. Small bureaucracies quickly surfaced in the form of local rating committees, invariably composed of participating sailors. The resulting conflict of interest makes objectivity impossible. Local rating committees are given the power of life or death over any boat's chances of success. They can and do often kill new designs by unrealistic ratings based on fear, prejudice, and ignorance. There is a way back to the sanity of the original concept. For a new or a contested rating, charge the applicant $100. Take a popular boat like the J/24, for which a wide performance sample ensures a fair rating. Let the applicant put the best crew he can find on the J/24, and the rating committee put their best crew on the applying yacht. Race a mile upwind together and a mile downwind. Repeat, and average the results. Adjust at year's end if discrepancies emerge. PHRF has to find a way to get politics out and let performance in. Picking a well-known benchmark measuring class would eliminate flagrant injustices and make observable performance the starting basis.

In my view, ratings are like welfare. Clothed in the noblest of intentions, they have proceeded to produce minor benefits at great cost and with damaging side effects. It is not that ratings haven't done any good. Of course they have. With ratings, people owning different kinds of boats have been able to race together in pleasing competition, and the results often truly reflect performance. The danger and the damage is the way ratings have added cost, incomprehensibility, and political chicanery to what the public already considered a dull and confusing spectator sport. *Ratings remove any possibility of the spectator grasping the essential ingredient for enjoying any sports competition—namely, the simple, observable knowledge of who is ahead.* Picture the following scene:

ANNOUNCER: "And the first boats are just finishing the Bermuda Race!"

SPORTS FAN: "Great—who won?"

ANNOUNCER: "Well, of course we won't know that just yet; these are just the first few boats finishing."

SPORTS FAN: "Don't the boats that finish first win?"

ANNOUNCER: "No. You see, it's a matter of ratings. The race committee has to multiply ratings by finishing times, and then they find out who wins the race."

SPORTS FAN: "Well, when will you know who won?"

ANNOUNCER: "In about two days, when all the smaller boats finish."

SPORTS FAN: "Two days?"

SPORTS FAN'S WIFE: "What does the winner get?"

ANNOUNCER: "Are we talking IOR or MHS?"

SPORTS FAN: "Ah. . . ."

ANNOUNCER: "There are two different divisions, you see. What class are you interested in?"

SPORTS FAN: "Ah. . . ."

ANNOUNCER: "You see there are a number of different classes—A, B, C, D, and E—and they each have their own winners."

SPORTS FAN: "Doesn't some one boat win?"

ANNOUNCER: "Well, there is an overall winner declared, but that usually depends strictly on whether it was big-boat weather or small-boat weather."

SPORTS FAN: "I think I'll stick to the horses."

If sailing insists on granting major importance to races whose results are determined by ratings, we will never achieve wide public interest because *ratings remove the vital pleasure of quickly observable results*. There can certainly always be a place for racing by ratings, but that place should not be center stage if we want to get this sport moving. The quicker we can shift the racing focus to events that allow people to see who is ahead and who wins, the sooner we will get more public interest. Here again, the boardsailors have shown the way with slalom events and races close to shore that the average person can enjoy and comprehend.

TWENTY

The World Champion Sailor

*T*he winner of the Olympic decathlon title is universally recognized and acclaimed as the world's best athlete, because the events involved in decathlon competition require all the prime elements of athletic skill—speed, strength, agility, and endurance. Everybody knows the decathlon champion is no fluke, and the event is perhaps the most dramatic and grueling single test of athletic versatility.

Sailing needs a similar title to create new public attention and to focus on the wide diversity of skills that go to make up sailing ability. All the events must be solo, for the same reason all the decathlon events are solo—to measure individual skill. There is a place for team efforts, but not in the determination of a single champion.

What kind of events would accurately define the world's best sailor? Well to begin with, such a champion must be able to demonstrate superiority in the world's most popular sailing styles, which I classify as:

1. Boardsailing
2. Dinghy sailing
3. Catamaran sailing
4. Distance sailing

I can envision a two- or three-day event culminating in an overnight ocean distance race that would test navigation and spinnaker skills. The choice of particular brand boats is not critical to the concept as long as all the boats are exactly the same, and as long as all the boats are designed specifically for singlehanding. For example, the boats could be:

1. Sailboard - Windsurfer
2. Dinghy - Laser
3. Catamaran - Hobie 14
4. Distance - Freedom 21

(Pardon my obvious prejudice in the latter class, but we do need a simple displacement boat with a cabin and bunk and a singlehanded spinnaker operation, and I can think of none better than the Freedom 21.)

While we are into prejudices, I might as well cite my preference for a race location like Newport, Rhode Island, which has the advantage of adjacency to both the ocean and the sheltered waters of Narragansett Bay. This means the first three events could be run in the bay, and the final ocean race could be an overnight contest around Block Island—starting and finishing in daylight for maximum viewer interest. But, again, the validity of the concept does not rest on any particular place or brand of boat; it is the idea that needs doing.

The winner of this new title, the "World's Best Sailor," is going to have to be first of all an athlete—the boardsailing category will see to that. But he or she can't be just some barefooted wave jumper, because the dinghy event will be won on tactical skills, the catamarans require special handling, and the overnight ocean race calls for navigation, endurance, and spinnaker handling. There is a tantalizing possibility that this title could be won by a woman, which would probably be the best thing the sport could hope for. But to assure female participation and interest, I would prefer to see a separate female championship run simultaneously. That would serve to vary the action and would also provide better utilization of the boats, which could be doubled up and made to serve both championships by simply alternating events.

The world sailing championship would be an annual event with commercial sponsors. Being able to focus on one single definitive champion (male and female) would give sailing some lead personalities for the public to identify with, something the sport now lacks. The event should be fully international, with each nation sending one representative and an international panel of referees. The event should be specifically designed to provide exciting TV viewing, with sailboard slaloms and short-leg dinghy races to assure lots of maneuvering action. The intent would be to make the event exciting and comprehensible to the average person, complete with TV close-ups of faces in action so people can know who they're rooting for or against and can follow the race tensions reflected in facial expressions.

This event would be a close-up chronicle of intense individual interaction with wind, sail, and water—the emphasis being on the people, not the equipment. In this sense it would be almost the exact opposite of an America's Cup competition, where the size, beauty, and complexity of the boats tends to overwhelm everything, and the rules allow only long-distance shots.

The competition for the World's Best Sailor would aim to go beyond the limited reach of the sailing press to include general sports page coverage. But television is the medium most needed to inject the sport with its yet unrevealed sense of combat excitement.

For this contest I would allow no protests. There would be a simplified rule structure, and penalties would be immediately assessed by expert referees watching from close quarters on the water and on TV screens. Nobody would get thrown out of the race, but penalty points would be leveled against infractions. For example, you could have ten-second, twenty-second, and thirty-second penalties, and these would be placed against the finishing times. If you won the race by nine seconds and had been earlier assessed a ten-second penalty, you would finish second. The assessment of penalties would be immediate, not delayed, and the TV audience as well as the competitors would be informed of the penalties by cards carried on referee boats. If certain infractions escape the referees—well, so be it—that happens in every sport. The point here is that to keep the excitement in, you've got to get the delays out. Again, we have to knock off some of the artificial (and unobtainable) purity we have tried to legislate onto the course.

There is absolutely no reason why small power launches steered by capable racing sailors cannot bring referees and TV cameras right into the midst of the sailing action. These small power launches would provide no more interference than football referees, or basketball referees, or hockey referees. And if they did get briefly in the way (as football, basketball, and hockey referees occasionally do), it would be a small price to pay for the benefit of clear, immediate penalties decided on the spot, plus being able to bring the public into the intimate excitement of the sport, which is a feeling you can only get by being right in there close.

I said earlier that no one would get thrown out of races. Let me amend that. If, during the competition, any competitor acted on or off the course the way John McEnroe is routinely allowed to act, the head referee should be empowered and instructed to throw his ass out on the spot—with no appeals granted.

An annual sailing championship conducted in these new terms, which allow exciting and comprehensible TV coverage, would be immediately attractive to alert commercial sponsors. The result could be the kind of intelligent mesh we need between commercial interests and the interests of the sport. The World Sailing Championship would not detract from any event that now exists, but would build wide new public interest in sailing.

TWENTY-ONE

The Business of Making Sailboats

*I*t can honestly be said that very few people understand it, probably least of all those who are engaged in it. (If they understood it, they wouldn't be in it!) First off, we're not really talking about a business; this is a cottage industry. After all, there are over two hundred "manufacturers" of sailboats doing "business" in the United States, each aiming for a share of a total annual market that can be roughly estimated at $300,000,000. To put this in perspective, the leading powerboat company individually does more annual dollar volume than the entire sailboat market. In terms of active participation, less than one percent of the U.S. population are sailors. You hear a lot of inflated numbers in this regard, but to get to the pathetic reality of the matter, examine the circulation figures for the four leading sailing magazines:

> *Sail* — 175,000
> *Cruising World* — 115,000
> *Yachting* — 145,000
> *Yacht Racing & Cruising* — 50,000

Even tripling these figures for family readership and ignoring the considerable overlap that exists among them, you come up with a total that is considerably less than one percent of the U.S. population. This analysis is reasonable, because it is fair to assume that anybody actively interested in a sport will seek to read something about it—particularly in a sport having a minimum cost of entry-level equipment of $1,000, and usually a lot more. Certainly anybody remotely interested in buying a boat would have to be interested in finding out what is available, and that is what the magazines provide.

There is a shortage of accurate production information in the sailboat business, but for the purpose of general discussion the aforementioned $300,000,000 annual market can be broken down into estimated shares by major U.S. manufacturers as follows:

Catalina — $40,000,000
Hunter — $25,000,000
O'Day   — $20,000,000
Pearson — $20,000,000
TPI   — $20,000,000

There is a second wave of about ten producers in the 10 to 15 million dollar annual sales vicinity, and then there is a sharp drop-off to a host of minor operators. The point of this informal and incomplete summary is not to get into an argument over who has more or less than the above numbers, but to show the elementary foolishness of a $300,000,000 market in which more than two hundred manufacturers compete with over 600 different models. Most of these 200 "manufacturers" make fewer than ten units per year—and that is a cottage industry in anybody's book.

Contrast this with the automobile industry, where only four U.S. manufacturers address a market that is vastly larger. The difference here of course is that it takes millions of dollars and years of preparation to get started in the car business, while all you need to get into the sailboat business is a garage, some resin, and an acute shortage of smarts. You can pick up molds for next to nothing, since sailboat builders go belly-up with amazing regularity. The stagnation of design progress means that ten-year-old molds still look about the same as the new models, and the result is a low entry fee that encourages a lot of people who have little more going for them than an enthusiasm for sailing.

The ensuing multiplicity of amateur manufacturers makes industry efficiency virtually impossible. Since the market is so small and fragmented, no single manufacturer ever gets enough volume to really achieve economies of volume. The result is very high unit prices for sailboats, an effect of low volume. The high prices are not because the manufacturers are making a lot of money—they simply don't. In fact, the profit rates for sailboat manufacturers are laughable in terms of other "real" businesses.

So the basic dilemma is a sailboat market that is too small and populated by too many manufacturers, and whose numerical presence makes it impossible for anybody really to succeed, and insures a high unit cost based on low volume. Since the high unit costs remain one of the chief obstacles to market growth, we can see another one of those circular situations in which the approach guarantees unsatisfactory results (like heavy keels that need tall rigs to drive heavy keels).

The already precarious lot of the U.S. manufacturer has been additionally complicated by the new entry of foreign producers, who now command approximately thirty percent of the market. The most successful importers are the French, whose prowess is based on the more intelligent structure of the boatbuilding business in France, where a small number of strong, local producers dominate the market. Beneteau, for example, is the world's largest sailboat manufacturer, and has reached volumes at which efficiency can begin to take hold. The Beneteau display at the Paris

Boat Show is a very professional operation, contrasting sharply with the amateur presentations of U.S. manufacturers in America. The Paris Boat Show is bigger and better than any U.S. boat show, and the Dusseldorf show in Germany is bigger than that. The French have clearly moved ahead in style and production technique, and most importantly in the structure of their national market. They *own* their own market (nobody sells into France). They have become efficient there, and now they can begin to ship that efficiency overseas. It has a Japanese ring to it.

The French first gained entry into the U.S. market on the artificially high strength of the U.S. dollar, which made their products almost ridiculously inexpensive in comparison with U.S. goods. The U.S. dollar has declined, mitigating that advantage, but the French builders are not likely to disappear from the U.S. marketplace. They are the only ones who have an intelligently structured domestic market, and because of that they have been able to marshal design, production, and marketing skills to a degree that no U.S. manufacturer matches. They are actively supported by their government, with export subsidies and tax exemptions that improve their export competitiveness.

These differences were directly dramatized to me this year when I saw President Mitterand of France visit the Paris Boat Show in order to officially open the Beneteau booth. Can you imagine President Reagan paying similar tribute to any U.S. sailboat manufacturer? Hell, we can't even get the U.S. Congress to force Canada to stop adding an exorbitant Canadian tax to U.S. boats at the border, while they continue to send Canadian boats into this market virtually tax-free.

The lot of the U.S. sailboat manufacturer is further complicated by an imposing array of negative factors:

1. The durability of fiberglass.
2. The increasing shortage of marina space.
3. A decline in entry-level sailing.
4. The high cost of advertising.
5. The high cost of boat shows.
6. Desultory design progress, which means that used boats continue to compete with new boats.

Let's look at these. Fiberglass boats, unlike cars, do not have the good grace to rust away and thereby clear the way for the sale of new products. Add design stagnation to this, and you have a particularly pernicious problem. From a structural point of view, a well-built twenty-year-old fiberglass hull is perfectly okay. If you Awlgrip away the faded gelcoat and buy a new mast, sails, blocks, and winches, you have for about one-half the cost a boat that compares in performance and appearance with the new models, because new design has failed to outdistance old design in any significant way.

U.S. sailboat manufacturers have yet to learn that when you produce a highly durable item, a special premium is placed on new design innovation, lest you find yourself competing with your own used boats.

By way of false solutions, U.S. manufacturers are currently caught up in the folly of annual cosmetic model changes. This involves expensive tooling costs for the sake of new appearance. The result is added expense, which keeps the cost of the boats high, thus maintaining the negative element that is the chief impediment to market growth. The average sailboat manufacturer's approach to design is to see what competitive model size and interior layout seems to be moving, and then rush to imitate that as quickly and as closely as possible. This creates a mishmash of intensely similar sloops, all saddled with high costs and no significant improvements.

Not every segment of the sailboat business is unprofitable. Some sailmakers, hardware manufacturers, sailing publications, and sailboat shows do quite well. Sailing publications are particularly profitable, which explains why there are so many of them in so small a field. In fact, sailing may be the only sport/recreation of which it can be said that the publications are the biggest businesses in the field.

Consider, for example, that *Cruising World* recently sold for a reputed $9,000,000. *Yachting* changed hands for approximately $26,000,000, which means that *Sail* magazine would be worth as much or more. I can assure you, there isn't a sailboat manufacturer in the country who could fetch more than $10,000,000 on the market. Pearson Yachts, long a flagship in the industry, recently sold for a reported $9,000,000, providing tangible evidence of comparable worth. When you consider that *Cruising World* has a staff of 35 plus a modest wooden building on lower Thames, and Pearson Yachts has over 280 people plus 60 acres on Narragansett Bay, a magnificent manufacturing plant, and a full line of designs and tooling, the contrast in return over investment is strikingly in favor of magazines over manufacturers.

Of course, the imports that so desperately threaten the U.S. builder are of no particular worry to the magazines; on the contrary, they merely represent a new source of advertising revenue, which, if anything, forces the domestic manufacturers to advertise more. Like good practitioners of the world's oldest profession, the magazines are impartially disposed to service either the defending or invading armies with equal ease and enthusiasm.

This does not make the magazines villains, it only makes them smarter (and notably richer) than the manufacturers who support them.

Boat shows are another costly expense to the manufacturer. It has become part of the prescribed wisdom of the sailboat business that appearances are mandatory at the Newport, Annapolis, New York, and Miami boat shows. And that's just the East Coast. This is a very expensive process that of course must be added to the already high cost of the sailboats. There is some peculiar inverted logic here. The manufacturers are providing the boats, which are the attraction that people pay to see at boat shows. So the manufacturers pay the boat show operators for the privilege of providing the attraction, which the boat show operators then charge the people to see. This is like having Frank Sinatra pay the nightclub instead of the nightclub paying Sinatra! Having collected money from the "talent" that the people are paying to see, the boat shows can then turn their attention to building the foot traffic that swells their gate receipts—the sale of hot dogs, beer, etc. Whether or not these boat show visitors have any intention of buying boats is not the boat show's concern at that point. As long as some business is done (which is inevitable) the charade continues to be promotable to the ever gullible sailboat manufacturers. And of course the excess number of manufacturers again creates an excessive number of boat show participants.

Here again, the boat show operators aren't villains. They have merely seen an opportunity, and, like any red-blooded American businessman, they are developing it. But a better way would be for the boat shows to charge the manufacturer (the talent) *less* and the visitors *more*. Their net dollars would stay the same, but the character of the shows would be more sensibly sales oriented. A standard visitor charge of $25 would in no way deter the serious buyer who is about to invest at least $10,000. Yes, it would probably stop the tire kicker who brings along his wife and three kids with dripping ice-cream cones. He's looking for an inexpensive day's outing, and the boat shows mistakenly provide that. Raising the visitor fee would reduce the traffic to serious customers and alleviate the overcrowded conditions that now make it difficult for the serious customer to freely circulate, compare products, and get serious about buying.

A more rational structure for the business of building sailboats would be to have about four strong U.S. producers who might control eighty percent of the market, and by virtue of that greater volume begin to achieve some economies of volume. This could begin to drive the cost of sailboats down instead of ever up. Lower sailboat costs would then generate an increased appeal to a wider audience, which would have the effect of expanding what is currently a contracting market. This could lead to more volume, which in turn could lead to better efficiency, which could further reduce prices.

Don't hold your breath. Builders are habitually the last to see the first thing they need—new and better designs. They equate cosmetic change with innovation, and mistake new models with progress.

The conservative nature of the sailboat customer doesn't help. The average sailboat customer has been steadily conditioned to be suspicious of change. Otherwise sensible people who wouldn't consider buying a car or a plane that looked as it did 30 years ago will put on their yachting blinders and balk if a sailboat *doesn't* look as it did 30 years ago. The sailing world needs to be awakened to the fact that innovation is not the enemy of tradition—it is a necessary source of new tradition.

Dealers handling both sail and power report a startling difference between the buying habits and attitudes of the two. The powerboat customer shows up, looks at the boat, asks how fast it will go and what it costs, and then either reaches for his wallet or walks away. Not so the sailboat customer, who badgers the dealer with a host of details, wants a demo sail, and then takes six months to make up his mind because he's out checking other dealers and other boats. Nor surprisingly, the dealers, many of whom are sailors, start to really like powerboats, and downplay sail.

Actually, it seems to have become a fact of life that successful sailboat builders must widen their base by developing entries into the growing powerboat business, because sailboat business by itself is too small and unsteady.

When you throw in the new product liability problems of our increasingly litigious society and the impossibility of obtaining product liability insurance, the sailboat builder emerges as an endangered species. The culprit and cause of this particular malaise is the lawyer's contingency fee system, which rewards greedy lawyers a lot more than helpless victims. England, for example, does not allow contingency fees, and sets a limit on how much a lawyer can earn or a jury can grant in liability suits. Unfortunately, the United States political system is riddled with lawyers, so prospects for relief and common sense are scant.

The sailboat building business in the U.S. is beleaguered. It's not big enough to command political attention and it is too diluted to develop the kind of organized clout needed to attack the basic problem of market growth and better control of costs.

Even the boardsailing segment—admirably equipped with a new and better idea—is not healthy at the builder level in the U.S. Again too many builders, and again, promoting the wrong image. Their overinsistence in showing supermen leaping upside down over waves can be likened to the hard-core IOR racers hanging ten men on the rail. Most of the public can't relate to that, and doesn't want to.

It is instructive to note that the leading sailboat manufacturer in the U.S., Catalina, does not advertise, and their participation in boat shows is handled largely by their dealers. Catalina boats are designed and built to carry the lowest prices in their size ranges; they don't pretend to be the highest quality, but they do deliver excellent value. This formula clearly works, because nobody comes close to Catalina in volume. This does not mean advertising is not effective, because it certainly is. In fact, Catalina cleverly encourages their dealers to handle other, *advertised* lines of boats. That way, they know, leads and traffic *developed by the advertised brands* will show up at their dealer's showroom, and that's when the Catalina price advantage goes to work. The Catalina sales success uses the proven reach of advertising to support their nonadvertising. *This tactic can only work when the general climate of marketing costs and manufacturing methods is not well tuned to market realities.*

And that is the point of this chapter. Not to throw a lot of blame around. That's easy, and just makes people mad. The problem is that sailboat manufacturers, magazines, and boat shows often seem to be working independently and at odds with each other. That may not be the intent of their behavior, but it is a result of their behavior. Consensus action against the core problem of developing more sailors, plus small adjustments in the way each sector does its business, could yield big improvements in which all would share. They are not independent, but extremely interdependent.

The people in the best position to help this situation, by virtue of their higher profitability and greater communications power, are the sailing magazines. They should take the lead with active steps to sponsor the new events and foster the new attitudes that are needed to expand the sailing market.

In the narrow sense, it is "not their job," but in the broader view, when the ship is sinking, everybody had better become a bailer—starting with the strongest guys.

TWENTY-TWO

Hard-a-Lee

*T*hose of you who have made it this far will surmise that I am restlessly discontent with the establishment's stultifyingly sterile approach to a sport whose origins were so refreshingly inquisitive. After all, it was sail that opened up the great geographic discoveries, and sea/sail power that decided much of the history which brought us to where we are. Should we then allow this exciting natural propulsion to wallow in a sargasso of stagnant design and declining public participation? How would that in any way serve the spirit of Columbus, Magellan, Drake, Nelson, or Perry? Better, I say, to opt for audacity and innovation—there is plenty of conformity around already.

It is neither likely nor desirable that you will agree with all my criticisms, or with all or any of my solutions. Some indeed may be put off by what they perceive to be self-serving promotion of my own ideas. Well, I can't help that. I'm vain enough to like my own ideas best, and they are the only ones I'm intimate enough with to fully explain. Let others explain theirs.

In my view the sport of sailing has been overdosing on caution, propriety, and artificial restraints. These are traits which I find to be out of character with the basically adventurous nature of seamanship. Sailing has been the dominant passion in my life, first as a racer, then as a cruiser, and now as a designer. For many pleasures received, I now owe candid comments. Foremost among these is my belief that in any field of endeavor there are always better ways to be found, and it is part of man's better instincts to seek them. Conventional wisdoms need to be periodically challenged to assure that they are wisdoms and not just practices hardened in place.

It simply cannot be right that sail, the working medium of the great explorers, should now be backwinded by rules, anchored by tradition, deviated by technology, and stranded for lack of daring.

What to do and where to seek? Well, had anyone said twenty years ago that the monohull sailing speed record would be over thirty-five knots, that it would be held by a man holding up a single sail on an eight-pound ski, and that this style of sailing would have more followers than any other, no one would have even remotely believed. Yet that is now the case. To appreciate the extent of that change, contemplate that the titles both of this book and its last chapter are meaningless, obsolete commands on the world's most popular sailboats. Be it by luck, or pluck, or genius, or guesswork, the Windsurfer kind of breakthrough is out there now, beckoning. It is a designer's treasure hunt, and I hold that fortune favors the bold, just as it ducks the timid and rebuffs the preposterous.

A number of years ago, I rode out the fringes of a hurricane in Trellis Bay, British Virgin Islands, aboard a Freedom 33. Exulting in my unscathed survival and in the bottle of wine imbibed in subsequent celebration, I penned the following:

> There's a ship that waits to take us
> Up the shimmering path to the sun
> Where there's time for dreams long forgotten
> And each wave has yet to be won

In the best tradition of literature, I now freely ascribe to the lines a meaning and significance the author never considered at the time. To wit:

There are wondrous sailing ships lying in the hidden coves of many minds. These dormant dreams derive from lessons learned in past ships, but will not be confined to those forms. And the moment any one of these latent schemes breaks out, whole ranges of new possibilities will unfurl. Such ideas prosper by inductive rather than deductive reasoning, and will amount to pole vaults of imagination that shortcut the normal, slow course of evolution. This is not necessarily a task for engineers, who tend to be walled in by what they know will work. Venturing forth on the chances of what might work is more rewarding than confirming the certainty of what we already know has worked, and it is the only way to unfetter imaginations.

So saying, by your leave I shall take my leave, hoping that graceful exit lines will make the smooth wake that is every designer's wish.

> *There's a shadow 'neath the surface*
> *Out past Matagorda Shoals*
> *You have to be there at a certain Island time,*
> *The sun must be set to angle past the reef,*
> *The tide just deciding which wave to come behind.*
>
> *Then with luck you'll see the outline,*
> *Was she sloop or schooner bold?*
> *The wreck they say has long been there,*
> *From the rhyming tales old sailors told.*

The divers scoff and say it's coral
Just rock that grew in a funny shape,
Looks more like a fish, or maybe a bird,
And whoever saw a boat like that?

But could it have been some early man
Not trained to know what couldn't be done,
Fashioned a ship from his mind's eye alone,
And sailed her swifter than ever was known?

So fast she lifted clean out of the sea
Poised like a dolphin arched at the blue,
So fast she broke and dived deep below,
Where she waits for the future to make her come true.

"The Swiftest Sailor"
Garry Hoyt